More Sensible Thinking

More Sensible Thinking

Martin H. Levinson

INSTITUTE OF GENERAL SEMANTICS

New York

First printing

Cover & Interior Book Design by Scribe Freelance

ISBN: 978-0-9827559-6-9

LIBRARY OF CONGRESS CATALOGING-IN-PUBLICATION DATA

Levinson, Martin H., 1946-
  More sensible thinking / Martin H. Levinson.
    p. cm.
  Includes bibliographical references and index.
  ISBN 978-0-9827559-6-9
1. Semantics (Philosophy) 2. Thought and thinking. I. Title.
  B840.L455 2012
  149'.94--dc23
                            2012036084

To Sanford I. Berman, Allen Flagg, Harry Maynard, and Frank Scardilli

CONTENTS

Acknowledgments

Thank you: to the trustees and directors of the Institute of General Semantics and New York Society for General Semantics for your diligent efforts in promoting and preserving Alfred Korzybski's general system of evaluation; to Bill Petkanas, the editor of *ETC: A Review of General Semantics*, for your excellent stewardship in keeping *ETC* one of the premiere journals around; to Neil Postman, my doctoral dissertation advisor at NYU and an ardent supporter of GS, for showing me that "crazy talk and stupid talk" can be minimized through diligent effort at minding one's language; to Harry Maynard, whose course in how to improve your thinking and communicating ability at Cooper Union introduced me to the field of general semantics; to Sanford I. Berman, Allen Flagg and Frank Scardilli, three excellent GS role models; to my mother, Professor Risha Levinson, the first author in our family; and to Katherine Liepe-Levinson, my wife and fellow writer, whose consistent support, advice, and encouragement sustained me in the completion of this project.

In addition, I need to thank the Institute of General Semantics, which has given me permission to reprint in a slightly different form the following pieces that have been published in *ETC: A Review of General Semantics*: "People in Quandaries: Sixty Years Later," *ETC* 63, no. 3 (July 2006): 290-298; "Crazy Talk, Stupid Talk—Redux," *ETC* 63, no. 1 (January 2006): 67-76; "Examining Five 'Over/Under-Defined' Terms Used in American

Political Discourse," *ETC* 65, no. 2 (April 2008): 134-140; "Science Versus Religion: A False Dichotomy?," *ETC* 63, no. 4 (October 2006): 422-429; "General Semantics And . . .," *ETC* 67, no. 2 (April 2010): 127-143; "Alfred Korzybski and Rational Emotive Behavior Therapy," *ETC* 67, no. 1 (January 2010): 55-63; "General Semantics and Emotional Intelligence," *ETC* 65, no. 3 (July 2008): 243-251; "General Semantics and Media Ethics," *ETC* 64, no. 3 (July 2007): 255-260; "Examining Ten Commonly Accepted Verbal Maps of American History," *ETC* 66, no. 4 (October 2009): 364-370; "A General Semantics Analysis of the *RMS Titanic* Disaster" *ETC* 69, no. 2 (April 2012): 141-156; "Mapping the Persian Gulf Naming Dispute," *ETC* 68, no. 3 (July 2011): 279-287; "Albert Schweitzer and Alfred Korzybski: Twentieth-Century Champions of Humanity," *ETC* 66, no. 1 (January 2009): 84-90; "How Science Should be Done: Insights From Santiago Ramón y Cajal," *ETC* 68, no. 1 (January 2011): 56-62; and "Your Most Enchanted Listener: GS Wisdom from Wendell Johnson," *ETC* 65, no. 4 (October 2008): 337-342.

Introduction

Six years have passed since the publication of *Sensible Thinking for Turbulent Times*, a book based on the formulations of general semantics (GS) that aimed to improve its readers' thinking abilities, emotional self-management, and analysis of social issues. In that interlude, the times have become more turbulent, which means there is even more of a need for sensible thinking. And so I give you *More Sensible Thinking*, a volume that like its forerunner offers GS tools and practical wisdom to sharpen one's ability to understand, manage, and surmount a world in flux.

General Semantics: An Effective Problem-Solving Approach

In the early part of the twentieth century, Alfred Korzybski, a trained engineer and a keen observer of the human condition, noted that scientists have great success solving technological problems and uncovering the mysteries of nature, while the nonscientific community has a poor record dealing with psychological and social issues. To improve the situation, Korzybski developed a science-oriented "self-help" system to help individuals and groups make more intelligent decisions in all aspects of their lives. He called this system *general semantics*.

A wide variety of writers, educators, therapists, and other professionals have drawn on and added to his system. Notable

1

contributors include: Steve Allen, polymath and writer of numerous books, including *Dumbth: 81 Ways to Make Americans Smarter* (idea number 81 is to learn general semantics); Alvin Toffler, author of *Future Shock*; Albert Ellis, originator of Rational Emotive Behavior Therapy; former US Senator S. I. Hayakawa, a student of Korzybski; and Neil Postman, founder of the media ecology program at NYU.

Many books have been published using general semantics to analyze and solve problems in areas such as education, communication, negotiation, management, social science, journalism, and personal adjustment. In addition, numerous articles on the benefits of general semantics have appeared in the *General Semantics Bulletin* and *ETC: A Review of General Semantics*, and more than 150 doctoral- and master's-degree studies have demonstrated its worth. General semantics is clearly a highly pragmatic discipline with a proven record of analyzing situations and solving problems.

Who Should Read *More Sensible Thinking*?

More Sensible Thinking will appeal to general readers interested in improving their problem-solving abilities, as well as to college students, therapists, educators, employers, employees, politicians, leaders, thinkers, and others. It offers practical ways to gather information more accurately, evaluate it more clearly, and act upon it more successfully. While the book can be profitably perused in its entirety, each of the chapters can also stand alone. This means every chapter can be understood without the need to read preceding chapters.

Outline of The Book

Like its predecessor, *More Sensible Thinking* contains fourteen chapters divided into four parts:

Part I offers a variety of methods to solve personal problems, reveals how applying general semantics can improve the way we think and talk, explores the limitations of language in political discourse, and questions the notion that science and religion must conflict.

Part II provides evidence of the beneficial effects of GS in diverse fields, discusses how GS formulations can help one to be more emotionally intelligent, looks into various connections between general semantics and rational emotive behavior therapy, and considers GS ideas and their relevance to journalism ethics.

Part III examines ten commonly accepted myths of American history, provides a general semantics analysis of the *RMS Titanic* disaster, and shows that words mean different things to different people.

Part IV reviews the lives and philosophies of Albert Schweitzer and Alfred Korzybski, furnishes commentary on the scientific method from Spanish physician and Nobel laureate Santiago Ramón y Cajal, and investigates material contained in *Your Most Enchanted Listener,* a book by Wendell Johnson that describes the efficacy of the scientific method and general semantics to solving problems of everyday life.

Chapter Summaries

Part I—The Map Is Not the Territory: Words Are Not the Things They Represent

Chapter 1, "People in Quandaries: The Semantics of Personal Adjustment," offers a brief overview and discussion of selected key points in *People in Quandaries,* Wendell Johnson's best-selling GS classic on overcoming personal troubles.

Chapter 2, "How We Defeat Ourselves by the Way We Talk—And What to Do About It," which is based on Neil Postman's book *Crazy Talk, Stupid Talk,* demonstrates how applying general semantics can improve the way we think and talk.

Chapter 3, "Over/Under-Defined Terms in American Politics," explores five expressions commonly used in American political discourse and shows that when it comes to the language of governance, the map is not the territory.

Chapter 4, "Science Versus Religion: A False Dichotomy," uses the GS technique of dating and historical examples from Western science and Western Christianity (the predominant religion in the Western world) to question the idea that science and religion must be in conflict.

Part II—Sensible Thinking for "Real World" Problems

Chapter 5, "Practical GS Applications" provides evidence showing that general semantics is a highly useful methodology with a wide range of applicability in diverse areas of human endeavor.

Chapter 6, "General Semantics and Rational Emotive Behavior Therapy," probes various connections between general semantics and rational emotive behavior therapy.

Chapter 7, "General Semantics and Emotional Intelligence," considers some of the key biological and theoretical underpinnings that support the concept of emotional intelligence and shows how the tools and formulations of general semantics can help a person raise their *EQ.*

Chapter 8, "General Semantics and Journalism Ethics," examines a number of GS ideas and their relevance to journalism ethics.

Part III—Going Beyond Similarities to Discover Differences that Make a Difference

Chapter 9, "Checking Conventional Maps of American History," underscores the view that conventional wisdom is not always correct.

Chapter 10, "A General Semantics Analysis of the *RMS Titanic* Disaster," applies GS formulations to investigate one of the most famous maritime tragedies in history.

Chapter 11, "Sorting Out the Persian Gulf Naming Dispute," utilizes the example of the Persian Gulf naming dispute to show that words mean different things to different people, words mean different things at different times, and words mean different things in different contexts.

Part IV—Practical Wisdom from Notable Thinkers

Chapter 12, "Albert Schweitzer and Alfred Korzybski: Champions of Humanity," reviews the lives and philosophies of Albert Schweitzer and Alfred Korzybski, two champions of humanity who devoted themselves to alleviating human suffering and advancing human welfare.

Chapter 13, "How Science Should be Done: Insights from Santiago Ramón y Cajal," presents observations on the scientific method from Spanish physician and Nobel laureate Santiago Ramón y Cajal, a seminal figure in the field of neuroanatomy.

Chapter 14, "GS Wisdom from Wendell Johnson," looks at material contained in *Your Most Enchanted Listener,* a book by Wendell Johnson that highlights the functional uses of general semantics in everyday life.

PART 1

The Map Is Not the Territory:
Words Are Not the Things They
Represent

1

People in Quandaries: The Semantics of Personal Adjustment

Wendell Johnson worked tirelessly throughout his life to create understanding of the processes of language and speech production. He developed a university-level course on general semantics, and it became one of the most popular courses at the University of Iowa, where he was a professor. He wrote more than 150 articles and nearly as many clinical and theoretical papers on the subject of language. And he published ten communications-related books, including *People in Quandaries: The Semantics of Personal Adjustment*—which was a best seller for several years.

I was introduced to *People in Quandaries* in 1979 in an adult education course taught by IGS trustee Harry Maynard titled "How to Improve Your Thinking and Communicating Ability" (the course really should have been called "General Semantics 101"). Maynard assigned several chapters in the book over the length of the semester, but I found Johnson's ideas and writing style so compelling that I finished the text in the first month of the term. In the remaining weeks, Johnson's clear and engaging critiques on the usefulness of general semantics to solve problems of everyday living motivated me to read other GS classics, like Irving J. Lee's book *Language Habits in Human Affairs* and *Language in Thought and Action* by S. I. Hayakawa. I was determined to learn as much as I could about general semantics.

8

I recently reread *People in Quandaries* and found, more than sixty years after it was originally published, its advice and relevance for solving personal problems still superb. I was moved by the profundity of Johnson's thoughts, the elegance of his writing, and the excellent examples he used to illustrate the practicality of general semantics for quotidian life. I hope when you finish this overview of some of the key points in *People in Quandaries*, you will come to the same positive conclusions as I did regarding this venerable work. (The quoted remarks that follow are from *People in Quandaries*. The subheads are chapter titles from the book.)

A Brief Overview of *People In Quandaries*

Introduction

"This is a book about the problems we have in trying to live with ourselves and with each other. These problems, together with ways of dealing with them, are discussed from the point of view of general semantics. This point of view emphasizes those aspects of the scientific method that are useful in daily living."[1]

Verbal Cocoons

Wendell Johnson was a counselor and teacher who spent much of his energy helping individuals to overcome their personal maladjustments. He observes such maladjustments often develop in people who are "frustrated and distraught idealists." They suffer from, what he termed, the *IFD disease*—failure to achieve high goals or ideals (the "I") leads to frustration (the "F"), and after sufficient repetition, to demoralization and depression (the "D").

Johnson finds the ideals of "maladjusted individuals" problematic in three important respects: (1) they are

9

mathematically unlikely to be reached (e.g., the woman who wants to be a movie star in feature films or the man who wants to make a million dollars a year by the time he is twenty-five); (2) they are very highly valued, so that one is devastated when they are not achieved (e.g., failing to become a member of a sorority or to make partner in a law firm); and (3) they involve words with no external referents, or means of measurement—they are vague (e.g., the person who wants to be successful, wealthy, beautiful, popular, famous, or powerful).

Because maladjusted people are idealists, they subject themselves more or less continuously to experience "failure" and so develop feelings of inferiority. "Now, what these people have not learned is the simple fact that there is no failure in nature. Failure is a matter of evaluation. Failure is the felt difference between what you expect and what you get."[2]

Johnson maintains that the personal quandaries we experience are like verbal cocoons in which we elaborately encase ourselves, and from which, we do not tend to hatch. "The particular structure of these cocoons appears to be determined in great measure by the structure of the society in which they are formed—and the structure of this society has been and continues to be determined significantly by the structure of the language which we so unconsciously acquire and so unreflectively employ. Simply by using that language and by living in terms of the basic orientation which it represents and fosters, we tend to cultivate the idealism and so to suffer from the frustration and demoralization which are so conspicuous in the lives of people in quandaries."[3]

Maladjusted people are often unable to clearly describe what their problem is. Some talk a great deal, with an impressive verbal output, but never get outside their verbal circles. Others say very little, because they do not know how to express what they think

and feel. Whatever the case, a general characteristic of maladjusted people is they have difficulty in specifying questions in such a way as to produce answers that would be relaxing, satisfying, and "adjustive."

An important characteristic of maladjusted people is they ask vague questions. Such questions cannot be answered with precision because the terminology of the question determines the terminology of the answer. Johnson notes that, "The particular questions we ask ourselves determine the kinds of answers we get, and the answers we get make of our lives, in large measure, the sort of lives they are."[4] To improve the kinds of answers we get, and so improve our quality of life, Johnson recommends learning general semantics.

Never the Same River

The Greek philosopher Heraclitus asserted, over two thousand years ago, that one cannot step in the same river twice. In saying this, he was going beyond the assertion that no two things are exactly alike, to the idea that no one thing is ever twice the same. He was expressing a process-character view of reality, which is a foundational idea to science and general semantics.

Although change is a fact of life, many people resist it. A key reason for this is that our culture teaches us to heed and respect similarities over differences. This tends to produce sweeping generalizations—such as, you can't change human nature; like father, like son; you get what you pay for; etc. Exceptions to the rule get swept under the rug with the assertion that they "prove" it. For the most part, people seek evidence to back up their generalizations.

But "Once we begin to look for differences instead of similarities, it is practically impossible to retain intact, or at all, our generalizations, beliefs, assumptions, etc. It is almost impossible, that is, not to get new ideas. For the habit of asking 'How do these things differ?' or 'How might this be different?' is one of the basic techniques of originality and creativeness. And it is just such a habit that is required for optimal adjustment to a reality of process, change, flux with its consequently incessantly occurring differences."[5]

The scientific method, a policy of subjecting "the word" to the test of experience and revising it accordingly, is an excellent technique to detect differences in things. That was shown in 1514 when Galileo climbed to the top of the leaning tower of Pisa and performed one of the first deliberately executed scientific experiments, in which he demonstrated that a heavy cannon ball drops no faster than a lighter one. Since then, science has led the way to immense technological progress in our ever-changing world.

General semantics may be regarded as a systematic attempt to formulate the general method of science in such a manner that it might be applied not only in the arena of professional science and technology, but *generally* in daily life. "It belongs, thus, in a tradition of Galileo and Newton and Maxwell, of Darwin and Pasteur and Pavlov, of Peirce and Russell and Einstein—of Heraclitus—the tradition of breaking traditions as a changing reality and changing humanity require."[6]

Science and Personality

"Calling it [the general method of science] common sense might be a mistake. It is simple sense, but it may not be very common. It tends to be very obvious—once stated or demonstrated. It is so obvious that one has to be extremely careful not to ignore it. Scarcely anything is more difficult to learn than something that is obvious. It is very much like trying to learn nothing at all, and it requires tremendous alertness to learn nothing. For example, most people, according to experienced swimming teachers, find it very difficult to learn how to float—apparently because there is nothing to learn. You don't do anything in order to float. What you have to learn is to do nothing that would keep you from floating. Learning general semantics—learning, that is, how to be scientific . . . is very much like that."[7]

"In addition to the unlearning or forgetting that is usually required of the student of general semantics, or of scientific method, there is demanded of him . . . much learning of the obvious. There are two common reactions that we tend to make to whatever we label as obvious. The first is that we feel we have always known it, since it is difficult to believe that we could have overlooked it. The second is that we feel that it must be not important, because it is so easy to 'understand.' In either case we tend to brush it aside, to spend any if little time pondering over it, and so we miss its implications."[8]

Science and Tomorrow

The following observation has even more relevance today than when Johnson made it more than sixty years ago. "Between nations and groups of nations, within nations, and *within individuals* in every quarter of the globe there is going on a tremendous and turbulent conflict. New ideals, new beliefs, new methods and ways of life are challenging old ideals and beliefs, old methods and ways of life. The old is prescientific and authoritarian; the new is scientific [and characterized by inquiry into the attributes of people and things]."[9]

Johnson on *science and judicial interpretation*: "The scientifically oriented person understands that what the Judge calls the voice of The Law is simply the Judge's own interpretation of the facts of the case at hand and of statements that other men have made . . . conscious of projection in himself and in others, [he] realizes very well that the voice of the Judge is indeed the voice of the Judge himself."[10]

With respect to effective living, as we predict, so we adjust to reality. "[But] false knowledge and false assumptions make for false predictions . . . Errors in prediction frequently incur physical injury, sometimes death. In the social realm they occasionally lead to depressions, widespread unemployment, international frictions, and wars."[11] To counter prediction-error, Johnson recommends using a scientific orientation, as the making of accurate forecasts is a recognized objective of the scientific approach.

The World of Not-Words

"In a basic sense a fact is an observation. An observation is the act of an individual. So it is that a fact is a personal affair . . . that is why a fact (considered as a personal observation) is necessarily incomplete: The individual who observes it is limited in observational capacity. And that, in part, is why a fact changes: The individual who observes it is himself changing continuously, and so he observes differently from time to time."[12]

Like facts, word definitions are also inevitably incomplete. "People who are accustomed, for example, to look in the dictionary for the meanings of words proceed under a great delusion if they suppose that what they find in a dictionary is a word's full meaning. What they find is that the dictionary definition of a word consists of other words. Moreover, a dictionary is a closed system. In it, not only is a word defined in other words, but these, in their turn, are also defined in other words—and if you follow far enough this trail of definitions of words, you find that it is a trail that goes in a great circle, so that finally you make the enlightening discovery that the words are defined by each other."[13]

The World of Words

"One of the advantages of writing over speaking lies, as a matter of fact, in the increased awareness of language that writing involves. At least, language that is written is not so likely to be forgotten, and it is not so likely to be uncritically accepted, as is language 'writ in the water' of speech. Certain primitive societies have managed to achieve rudimentary forms of culture and to survive for centuries without written language, but no advanced civilization was possible until the invention of writing and other methods of making more or less permanent records of symbolization, such as painting, geometry, and other mathematics, etc. Professor John Dewey once declared that the invention of symbols was the outstanding event in human history."[14]

"The crucial point to be considered in a study of language behavior is the relationship between language and reality, between words and not-words. Except as we understand this relationship, we run the grave risk of straining the delicate connection between words and facts, of permitting our words to go wild, and so of creating for ourselves fabrications of fantasy and delusion . . . It is also to be recognized that by far the greater part of what we communicate to others in the form of language is not words about facts in a direct sense; rather, it is predominantly made up of words about words. Firsthand reports of direct experience comprise a relatively small proportion of the speech of most of us."[15]

The words we use can fool us. "Because the words we speak today are quite the same as the ones we spoke yesterday, we tend to create the illusion that what we speak about is also quite the same. It can be serious enough when change takes us by surprise; what is even more serious is to have change escape our notice entirely. That is the condition of persistent delusion."[16]

The Process of Abstracting

"Translated into the language of general semantics . . . [Professor R. D. Carmichael's statement that the universe, as known to us, is a joint phenomenon between the observer and the observed] says that the process of abstracting is personal, private, and projective. The moment you say of any word or statement, or any object, that it constitutes an abstract, you imply that it is abstracted *from something by someone*. The words 'by someone' represent the fact that an abstract is personal or private . . . And if abstracting is a personal process it must also be projective."[17]

"In science as general method, at its best, the process of abstracting is cleared of semantic blockages and proceeds freely. Under such conditions it is self-corrective . . . Any theory, assumption, belief, opinion, etc., is automatically referred back to reality to be tested against relevant observations and experience, and to be corrected accordingly. In this sense, any *scientific* theory contains the seeds of its own revision. That is why scientists are 'always changing their minds.' A scientific 'truth' is always tentative, subject to change in accordance with the further observations to which it invariably directs us."[18]

The Language of Maladjustment

"It is worth special comment that, while it is probably widely recognized that people who talk very little are likely to be not altogether well adjusted, it is not so generally understood that glibness is quite as significant in this respect . . . The very fact that in our culture a high value is placed on 'the gift of gab' accounts, in no small part, for the nervous striving for volubility which [*sic*] some persons exhibit. It accounts for the tendency of other individuals to lose confidence in their ability to speak acceptably and so become relatively quiet . . . In this connection, it is of more than minor interest that often one of the most noticeable effects of the study of general semantics is to be seen in a tendency to delay one's verbal reactions, and to talk less, more slowly, with less agitation and more accuracy—and so with greater self-assurance and general effectiveness."[19]

Human maladjustment is fostered by certain types of language rigidity. *Content rigidity* is to be seen in the range and variability of topics that one speaks about; *formal rigidity* in the degree of monotony of sentence form, style, word usage, etc.; and *evaluational rigidity* in the persistence of verbally expressed beliefs. Johnson offers the following as an example of evaluational rigidity.

"It has been reported of a certain British colonial governor in Africa that he had been having great difficulty keeping the natives under control. One day, however, a friend visited him, sized up the situation, and made a suggestion. With the governor's consent he ordered from London a generous supply of large pictures of Queen Victoria. When they arrived he placed them on the walls in all the native huts. The governor's difficulties ended as if by magic; the natives became very subservient. Bewildered, the governor asked his friend, 'Why on earth do these natives respond this way to a picture of Queen Victoria?' But his friend replied, 'Picture of Queen Victoria? Oh, no. To these natives it isn't a picture of Queen Victoria. It *is* Queen Victoria!'"[20]

Language as Technique
"Man has been called the talking animal. Man is not the same as an animal, of course, precisely because he does talk. Animals have their problems and their tragedies, but man seems

to be the only creature who can talk himself into difficulties that would otherwise not exist."[21]

One of those difficulties is coming up with a useful definition of "intelligence." "Alfred Binet, the creator of the modern intelligence test, stressed the significance of self-criticism in his attempts to define intelligence. The extent and the effectiveness of one's self-critical tendencies are to be seen particularly in the questions one asks, especially the questions one asks concerning the validity and the significance of one's own beliefs and attitudes."[22]

People in quandaries often have difficulty asking cogent questions. They also frequently exhibit other kinds of linguistic awkwardness. Johnson states, "The verbal ineptitude of people in quandaries is to be observed in extremes of verbal output; in content, formal and evaluational rigidity; in dead-level abstracting; and in the elementalism, the absolutism, and the either-orishness of the structure of the language they employ . . . With a fair amount of practice one can become reasonably skilled in observing these characteristics of language behavior in oneself and in others. The ability to recognize them gives one a measure of control over them, and a degree of insight into the basic mechanisms of adequate evaluation."[23]

Our Common Maladjustments

Johnson believes that aggression is in large measure a form of learned behavior. "This means that it is not something to be taken for granted as a fixed item in human nature. It is learned, as most other behavior is learned, simply to the extent that it gets results—and *to the extent that the individual recognizes no more effective means whereby he might obtain the same or more desirable results.* It is this latter consideration that is crucial, from a general semantics point of view. For there are more effective means than maladjusted aggression to get more desirable results than it produces."[24]

Mature individuals, and societies, do not instinctively resort to aggression to bring about the outcomes they want, and that is a good thing because impulsive aggression tends to produce negative consequences for all concerned. Surely, for the good of humankind and the survival of our species, it is important for people to behave in a mature manner. Johnson says this about achieving maturity: "For the normal adult the melody of childhood may linger on, but the song has ended; he does not permit the memory of early fears and affections to determine unduly his present conduct. He views his childhood as history, and he recognizes that evaluations and reactions adequate for him as an adult were neither necessary nor possible at the age of four. Growing up and achieving maturity for the individual is what the process of time-binding is for the [human] race. It is a matter of starting each new day not where yesterday began but where it ended."[25]

And So, Forth

"It is the distinctive contribution of general semantics that it formulates the *method* of science in a way that makes reasonably clear the possibilities of its application to our personal and social problems. It presents this method, in fact, as a design for living in the every day sense of the word. It attempts to cut through the bewildering overgrowth of elaborate theory and technicality, and so reveal the heartening simplicity of the few notions, principles, and techniques that make up the fundamentals of science."[26]

Johnson further states, "there is something almost bold in the proposition that the method of science not only provides a means of investigating personality, but also represents in itself the pattern of behavior that constitutes normal personality. That is the fundamental proposition of this book, and of general semantics. *The method of science is the method of sanity.*"[27]

2

How We Defeat Ourselves by the Way We Talk—And What to Do About It

In the 1970s, I worked as a junior high school counselor in New York City. The students at my school did not want to be in the building, the teachers were burnt out, and the administrators were bewildered about how to handle the situation.

Fortunately, I came across a book that helped me to understand what was going on, Neil Postman's *Crazy Talk, Stupid Talk: How We Defeat Ourselves by the Way We Talk and What to Do About It*, one of the best self-help texts ever written. Postman, a former editor of *ETC: A Review of General Semantics,* was the founder of the media ecology program at NYU. In *Crazy Talk, Stupid Talk,* he presents a philosophy of everyday language and describes different types of dysfunctional communication. He also shows how using general semantics can improve the way we think and talk.

Crazy Talk, Stupid Talk begins with this quote from Goethe: "One should, each day, try to hear a little song, read a good poem, see a fine picture, and, if it is possible, speak a few reasonable words." Neil Postman made a career of speaking and writing reasonable words. This chapter presents some of them.

Crazy Talk, Stupid Talk

Postman defines *stupid talk* as talk that has (among other

difficulties) a confused direction or inappropriate tone or a vocabulary not well suited to its context. It is talk that does not or cannot achieve its purposes. "To accuse people of stupid talk is to accuse them of using language ineffectively, of having made harmful but correctable mistakes in performance. It is a serious matter, but not usually dreadful."[1] A road sign that reads *No crossing the median divider* is an example of stupid talk, since it has the potential to confuse some drivers (the phrase "median divider" is the problem).

Postman asserts that *crazy talk* is almost always dreadful. "[it] is talk that may be entirely effective but which has unreasonable or evil or, sometimes, overwhelmingly trivial purposes. It is talk that creates an irrational context for itself or sustains an irrational conception of human interaction. It, too, is correctable but only by improving our values, not our competence."[2] Vandals who paint a "3" into an "8," so a road sign will read *Speed limit 85 miles,* are practicing crazy talk.

Semantic Environments

In Postman's view, human communication takes place in "semantic environments." Such environments include four elements: people, their purposes, the general rules of discourse by which such purposes are usually achieved, and the particular talk that is actually being used in the situation (the interaction of these elements would be labeled in general semantics parlance "organisms-as-a-whole-in-environments"). Science, religion, politics, commerce, war, sports, lovemaking, and lawmaking, among others, are examples of semantic environments. Let us take a closer look at two of them—religion and science.

The semantic environment of religion serves, at its best, to minimize fear and isolation and to provide a sense of continuity and oneness. Religious language achieves these purposes by creating metaphors and myths that give concrete form to our most profound fears and exaltations. Religious language offers a set of principles to give ethical purpose and direction to people.

In the semantic environment of science, one finds sentences that are mostly descriptive, predictive, and explanatory. Scientific language centers not on discovering true beliefs but on detecting those that are false. Scientific language provides a method to solve technical problems and problems of everyday living.

Purposes

There can be differences in the purposes of specific individuals in a situation and the purpose of the situation itself. Postman offers the following example of this state of affairs by referring to a *Peanuts* cartoon that gets to the heart of the matter.[3] Charlie Brown is screaming at Lucy because she made a stupid play in their baseball game: "You threw to the wrong base again!" Charlie cries. "There were runners on first and second and you threw the ball to first! In a situation like that, you always throw to third or home!" Lucy considers his advice and replies, "You're destroying my creativity!!" The problem is such creativity works against the purposes of baseball. For social order to be maintained, individuals need to follow the rules of structured environments.

Another source of conflict over purposes can occur when stated purposes do not match actual purposes. For example, a business leader says that he believes in honest competition, and then we find out that he has tried to win monopoly status for his company. Or a politician says that he is an advocate of tight budgets, and then he votes for tax cuts and more government spending.

A third source of conflict, somewhat similar to the above, can appear when the purpose of a semantic environment subverts the purpose of a subsystem within it. For instance, religion, in a broad sense, has as an overriding purpose—the "connectedness" of all people. Yet many religious practices, rituals, and institutions are motivated by the idea that people are morally different—some will have access to eternity and others won't. Much religious conflict stems from the idea of exclusiveness, while, paradoxically, "true" religious sentiment promotes the idea of inclusiveness.

Relationships

People tend to be highly sensitive to the rules of role structure. When such rules are broken, the consequences can be severe. For example, Postman recounts that when he was in the army all passes were cancelled at his base one weekend. A private in the barracks pleaded with the lieutenant to grant him a pass to see his girlfriend. The officer denied the request. The private then suggested the soldiers in the unit vote on the matter and that he would go along with the result. This suggestion, which was sincerely offered and delivered in modulated tones, led to additional punishments for the private. (Another example of role-structure naiveté: lecturing an IRS agent who is reviewing your income tax returns as if he were a child.)

The tendency of semantic environments to maintain their role structure is quite important since it provides us with a basis for predictable continuity in life. But it can also be seen as the source of cruel behavior. The famous Milgram experiment, in which people followed the orders of the experimenter to administer what they thought were electric shocks to others, is a case in point. At the end of his study, Milgram remarked that *relationship overwhelms content*—what people do is not as important as the "role" which asks them to do it.

Content

The words that comprise a semantic environment are not so much *about* a subject as they *are* the subject itself. To wit, subtract all the words that are used in discussing physics or law or theology, and you have just about subtracted those fields as disciplines. If there is nothing to talk *with*, there is nothing to talk *about*.

Words are the content of our thoughts. As the philosopher Ludwig Wittgenstein put it: Language is not only the vehicle of thought; it is the driver. Discussing what words to use in describing an event is not a matter of "mere semantics." It is about trying to control the perceptions and responses of others (as well as our own) to the character of the event itself.

This point is illustrated in the story of the three umpires. The first umpire, a man of little knowledge about how meanings are made, says, "I calls 'em as they are." The second umpire, knowing a bit about human perception and its limits, says, "I calls 'em as I sees 'em." The third umpire, a student of Wittgenstein, says, "Until I calls 'em, they ain't."

What you call something depends on how well and widely you see. If you are "locked into" a particular vocabulary of a subject, you will not be able to imagine alternative ways of conceiving it. You will thus be at the mercy of someone else's names and the purposes that such names imply. The more flexible you are in conceiving alternative names for things, the better you will be able to control your responses to situations.

Crazy Talk, Stupid Talk—Particular Characteristics

Fanaticism

Fanaticism is the internalization of sentences to which we are so attached that we have made them immune to criticism—not only by others, but by ourselves, as well. Put another way, fanaticism is what happens when we have no will to refute. Thus, our only protection from fanaticism is to develop and maintain our will to refute.

Karl Popper, a philosopher of science, has advanced a rational approach for refutation. He calls it "fallibilism"—a notion that presumes that all people and their ideas are fallible and that it is not possible for anyone to know if they are in possession of the "truth." Popper suggests we apply "critical rationalism" to one's beliefs by subjecting them to constant criticism in the hope of reducing the extent of their error. In Popper's view, the history of science is the history of detecting false beliefs, not the history of finding true ones.

Role Fixation

Stupid talk is the most characteristic symptom of role fixation—a condition in which a person cannot move from one semantic environment to another (e.g., the professor who always lectures in conversation, the comic who is constantly "on," cynics who never allow themselves to be awed, or let anything be revered). People who are fixated in roles may think they have "strong characters," but they can also be seen as single-dimensional without the courage to try out new roles.

Postman argues that health implies a capacity to grow and that semantic health cannot be acquired through mastering simple formulas for a single way of talking. While semantic flexibility has its limits—we probably don't want to be as chameleon-like as Woody Allen's Zelig—one measure of our ability is our competence in a wide range of semantic environments and social roles.

The IFD Disease

The *IFD disease*, a term coined by Wendell Johnson in his general semantics classic *People in Quandaries*, describes a condition in which high ideals combined with continued frustration can lead a person to become demoralized (IFD specifically refers to an individual going from ldealization to Frustration to Demoralization). It is a form of crazy talk because glorified ideals, such as "true happiness" or "real success," are vague standards that have no objective referents in the "real world."

The cure for IFD disease is to connect language with real and specific possibilities. For example, happiness is a warm onion roll with cream cheese on it; happiness is your car starting in the morning when the temperature is ten degrees. Or, if it is not these things, happiness must be something that you *do* or you can imagine yourself doing, something specific and achievable.

Model Muddles

In schools, tests are given to determine how smart someone is, or more precisely, how much smartness someone "has." If one child scores 140, and another 108, the first is thought to "have" more smartness than the other. But people don't have smartness. They "do" smart things and sometimes do stupid things—depending on the circumstances they are in, how much they know about the situation, and how interested they are. Smartness is not something you are, or have, in measurable quantities.

"Madness," like smartness, can be classified in particular ways. The *medical model* considers it a disease, the *moral model* looks at it as a character defect, and the *social model* views it as a product of a "sick society." Each metaphor invites an entirely different view of madness and as a result can expand our understanding of the subject. In discussing madness, or smartness, or any other abstract concept, it is important to know what metaphors are being used to avoid confusion, impotence, and bad temper that can arise from inadequate or partial models of "reality."

Reification

Reification means confusing words with things. The key grammatical instrument through which it is accomplished is the verb *to be*, and its variants. For example, when we say "She is lazy" or "He is smart," we are suggesting that "laziness" is found in her or that "smartness" is found in him. That contradicts what is really going on: we are projecting our opinions concerning "laziness" and "smartness" onto other people.

Another way we confuse words with things is to believe that words have "real" definitions. A definition is not a manifestation of nature, but a tool for helping us to achieve our purposes. To quote the British literary critic I. A. Richards: "We want to do something, and a definition is a means of doing it. If we want certain results, then we must use certain meanings (or definitions). But no definition has any authority apart from a purpose, or to bar us from other purposes."[4]

Poorly Reasoned Questions

A great deal of stupid and/or crazy talk is produced by poorly reasoned questions, sometimes spoken silently to ourselves, such as, "Why am I a failure?" and "What is the meaning of life?" These questions are formed at such a high level of abstraction that they cannot be reasonably answered. Another problem arises from certain structural characteristics of sentences. For example, many questions seem to limit responses to either-or alternatives—"Is that good?" "Is she smart?" "Is he rich?"

A third source of problems with respect to question-asking language is the assumptions that underlie it. Such assumptions can lead us into accepting as fact uncertain and even preposterous ideas. Two famous assumption-riddled questions are, "Have you stopped beating your wife?" and "How many angels can dance on the head of a pin?"

Finally, two people in the same semantic environment may ask different questions about a situation, but without knowing it. For instance, in a classroom, a teacher may be asking himself or herself, "How can I get the student to learn this?" But the student is probably asking, "How can I get a good grade in this subject?"

By-passing

By-passing, a term coined by general semantics expert Irving J. Lee, is a process in which the following occurs: A says something to B. B assumes that A means what B would have meant if B had said those words in that situation to A. Thus, there seems to be no reason to ask A, "What do you mean?" B can go straight to the question, "Do I agree or disagree?"

By-passing can be disastrous. For example, let's say A has said to B "I love you." The meaning of that sentence depends completely on the life experience of the person using it. B may be in for a rude awakening if she or he does not spend some time observing A's behavior and figuring out what A means when using the words "I love you." (A general semanticist might advise B that $love_1$ is not $love_2$, is not $love_3$, etc.)

By-passing is a "natural" form of stupidity that occurs because all communication is based, to some extent, on projection. We tend to become aware of by-passing only when people's actions are very different from what their words have led us to expect. A person who says "I love you" and then dates your best friend is not only creating a painful situation for you, he or she is teaching you the limitations of talking to yourself.

Sloganeering

Slogans are intended to go beyond reasoning with the hope of eliciting signal reactions (quick, unthinking responses, also called knee-jerk reactions). They are a form of groupthink that says "This is what *we* believe," not "This is what *I* believe." Slogans such as "Let's go, Mets!" and "On, Wisconsin!" are fairly benign with respect to having detrimental effects on individuals and societies. That cannot be said of slogans like "Sieg, heil!" and "Death to all infidels!"

In many semantic environments (e.g., religion, sports, politics) mindless recitation in the form of slogans is encouraged. Sloganeering is, in fact, practiced ubiquitously through pledges, oaths, banners, bumper stickers, college cheers, mantras— wherever it appears desirable to ease the burden of individual responsibility for thinking things through.

Postman argues that, generally speaking, when you find yourself applauding, cheering, or chanting in public places you may suspect that your intelligence has been by-passed, and that an individual or group is encouraging your signal reaction. Knowing this, you may wish to applaud, cheer, or chant because you want to "let go" or submerge yourself in a collective mood. But unless you know what is going on, and understand that you have an option to withdraw, you are taking part in a fairly dangerous exhibition of stupid talk.

Crazy Talk, Stupid Talk—And General Semantics

Postman ends his book with an "Autobibliography," a brief, highly personal commentary on nine books from which he says he has learned a great deal.[5] Two volumes on general semantics are included among the nine references: Alfred Korzybski's

Science and Sanity and Wendell Johnson's *People in Quandaries.* With respect to Korzybski's work, Postman writes, "Many academicians do not care for Korzybski—in part, because he is not careful, and in part, because they have no patience with genius."[6] As for Johnson's book, Postman says, "I am tempted to say that there are two kinds of people in the world—those who will learn something from this book and those who will not. The best blessing I can give you is to wish that as you go through life you be surrounded by the former and neglected by the latter."[7] These remarks, and the inclusion of *Science and Sanity* and *People in Quandaries* in his Autobibliography, show Postman's high regard for general semantics as a useful discipline for preventing crazy and stupid talk.

Over/Under-Defined Terms in American Politics

G eneral semantics views most terms as *over/under-defined*:
"They are over-defined (over-limited) by intension, or verbal
definition, because of our *belief* in the definition; and are
hopelessly under-defined by extension or facts."[1] Over/under-
defined terms are indeterminate in *extensional* (factual) meaning
until they can be specified extensionally through hard data.

This chapter will examine five over/under-defined terms
commonly used in American political discourse. In the process,
we will see evidence of another GS formulation. Specifically,
when it comes to language—and most things in life—*the map is
not the territory.*

Five "Over/Under-Defined Terms" Used in American Political Discourse

Undocumented Immigrant

There are an estimated twelve million illegal Mexican aliens
in the US, and their presence here has become a major political
issue.[2] Some assert they are doing jobs that Americans won't do,
so they should be welcomed into the country. Others say they are
taking jobs from Americans and pose a serious security threat.

In arguing this immigration issue, the term *undocumented immigrant* has been used to advance the case that favors relaxing restrictions on illegal immigrants coming from Mexico. The idea behind using this term is that it focuses on the bureaucratic aspect of the problem rather than on the criminal one, and so it is more likely to gain sympathy from the public and legislators to ease immigration rules than the term *illegal alien* would.

While arguments can be made both for and against loosening up restrictions on illegal immigration, nebulous language does not help in promoting a rational discussion of the issue. The fact is, sneaking across the border is illegal. Hiring those who come here like that is also illegal. And while we are certainly "a nation of immigrants," we are not a nation of illegal immigrants.

Many illegal aliens work "off the books" in the United States in low-level jobs. They risk being caught, detained, and deported; they often live in fear; and labor laws do not protect their rights. To remedy these, and other problems, many people have argued that our nation needs new immigration legislation.

Whether one is for or against such legislation, it is important that all sides talk and think "straight" about the issue of illegal immigration. One way to do that is to carefully examine the terms that are being used to describe people who are unlawfully coming into the United States.

Democracy

The word "democracy" is frequently in the news these days.[3] But that word is not so easily defined.

Historically, the term "democracy" has a checkered past going back to the Greek city-states. The Greeks defined democracy differently than we do now. For example, the citizens of Athens, the "demos," consisted of a privileged class that excluded women, slaves, farmers, and those who worked by the sweat of their brow.

The Romans did not particularly care for "democracy" in its suggestion of direct participation by the people. They used the word "republic" to describe a method of having senators, who were not indifferent to the "vox populi," elect consuls. The term "democracy" languished for many centuries but was revived in the 1600s when questions concerning the nature and foundation of the state assumed renewed importance. Thomas Hobbes, in *Leviathan* (1651), wrote that democracy in any form would eventually lead to anarchy. John Locke disagreed. In *Two Treatises on Government* (1689, 1690), Locke condemned hereditary power and advanced an idea that has attached itself to the word "democracy" to this day—the notion that "the beginning of politic society depends upon the consent of the individuals to join into and make one society."

In the eighteenth century, Locke's thoughts on what might be called a "democratic polity" were debated in Europe. Voltaire preferred an "enlightened monarchy." Denis Diderot favored a "constitutional monarchy." When the discussion about democracy transferred from Europe to America, the word was not accorded the respect we have for it today. Our nation's founders were divided over its meaning.

The word "democracy" does not appear in the Declaration of Independence or the federal Constitution. Thomas Jefferson in his first inaugural address said, "We are all Republicans, we are all Federalists;" he did not say, "We are all democrats." Alexander Hamilton and John Adams used the term in a pejorative sense. The Founders preferred a Roman conception of republicanism to the Greek "democracy." (In America's beginnings, citizens did not directly vote for president, vice-president, or members of the Senate. It should also be remembered that blacks and women did not receive full suffrage rights when the Constitution was adopted.)

In the twentieth century, despots like Benito Mussolini, Adolf Hitler, and Josef Stalin, used the word "democracy" to praise the tyrannies they headed. Today, other dictators use the term to describe their regimes. But for those of us in the developed world, the word "democracy" has taken on a more or less settled meaning. Its key aspect is the freely given consent of the governed to abide by the laws and policies of those agencies whose activities control the life of a community. (How that consent is given expression and by whom is usually defined by a constitution, which is subject to amendment.) To ensure that those who have given consent have done so without duress and in a considered manner, freedom of thought and speech must be given the widest latitude.

When he was in office, President George W. Bush argued that democracy, in the way we use that term, would move the Iraqi people to have happier and more productive lives. Maybe that will eventually prove true. But maybe people who have been conditioned to accept orders from fundamentalist clerics have a different conception of democracy. Maybe they believe, like America's founding fathers and the citizens of ancient Athens, that it is within proper democratic bounds to restrict the rights of women and other groups of people. Time will tell which definition of democracy will prevail.

War on Drugs

The phrase *War on Drugs* oversimplifies the "drug problem" by suggesting that all drugs can be divided into two mutually exclusive categories, "good and bad" or "safe and dangerous." There is a tendency to view drugs so categorized as similar, if not equivalent, and to make policy based on that idea. Drugs labeled as dangerous and whose use has been declared illegal are grouped together as "bad drugs," and distinctions among them are minimized, despite the fact that they almost always include substances that are diametrically opposite in their action. Alcohol and tobacco, two substances that are legal in many countries, often escape serious scrutiny because they are not even thought of as drugs.

The term War on Drugs obfuscates the fact that there are three basic elements in the use of any drug, legal or illegal, medical or non-medical: (a) the substance; (b) the individual who uses it; and (c) the social and cultural context in which the use occurs. Most drug-problem analysts agree that any effective approach to the drug problem needs to take in all three factors. Action based exclusively on one is likely to fail. Also, each of the aforementioned elements is complex and the relative degree of complexity with which it is perceived usually depends on the experience, background, training, and personal or professional investment of the viewer.

Individuals who work in drug prevention, treatment, law enforcement, and drug policy roles tend to agree that ignoring or distorting any one of the three basic elements previously described makes modification of drug-using behavior less than effective. But such intricate thinking goes against a human tendency to define problems in such ways that they are amenable to easy resolutions, especially ones that a given group is prepared to provide.

H. L. Mencken said, "There is a solution to every problem, quick, simple, and wrong."[4] Perhaps a more wide-ranging approach to solving the drug problem than the one we are currently using might get this bio-psycho-social crisis "right."

Affirmative Action

Affirmative action, a policy that generally means giving preferential treatment to minorities in admission to universities or employment in government and businesses, was originally developed to correct decades of discrimination and to give "disadvantaged minorities" a boost. The diversity of our current society, as opposed to that of sixty years ago, seems to indicate this policy has been a success, and many currently think affirmative action is no longer needed and that it leads to more problems than it solves.

One notable example is *Gratz v. Bollinger* (2003), a case argued in the Supreme Court concerning admission to the University of Michigan. The school had a procedure of rating potential applicants on a point system. Being a minority student earned you more than twice as many points as achieving a perfect SAT score. Three white students sued, citing this as race-based discrimination. School officials said that diversity is desirable and affirmative action is the only way to achieve true diversity. Several other cases involving affirmative action have observed similar lines of reasoning.

Those who are for affirmative action say that diversity is desirable and won't always occur if left to chance; that students starting at a disadvantage need a boost; that affirmative action draws people to areas of study and work they might not consider otherwise; that affirmative action is needed to compensate minorities for centuries of slavery or oppression; and that some stereotypes may never be broken down without affirmative action.

Opponents of affirmative action argue that it leads to reverse discrimination; that it lowers standards of accountability needed to push students to perform better; that students admitted on this basis are often not equipped to handle the schools to which they've been admitted; that getting rid of affirmative action would help lead to a truly color-blind society; and that success is labeled a result of affirmative action rather than on hard work and ability.

Those who favor affirmative action see it as a virtuous, optimistic, forward-moving program. Those opposed to it view in an opposite way. So, is affirmative action a beneficial and constructive policy? The answer to that question would seem to depend on how one chooses to characterize affirmative action.

The PATRIOT Act

Congress passed the USA PATRIOT Act (Uniting and Strengthening America by Providing Appropriate Tools Required to Intercept and Obstruct Terrorism) in 2001, just weeks after the 9/11 attacks, to help law enforcement work more effectively in investigating potential terrorists.

The legislation's acronym, "USA PATRIOT," suggests that the act is about being patriotic, that is, about being devoted to and protecting America. But there are some patriots who oppose the legislation. (*The American Heritage Dictionary* defines *patriot* as one who loves, supports, and defends one's country.) They maintain that the PATRIOT Act does more harm than good. To get a better handle on the legislation, let's go beyond its label and look at some of the arguments that have been made for and against the law.

Arguments For the PATRIOT Act

A number of Americans favor the PATRIOT Act because they believe it has increased national security in these perilous times. More specifically, they say the Act reduces terrorists' ability to operate within the United States by allowing law enforcement to access information such as bank statements, library records,

38

and emails without notifying individuals of the search. Supporters also claim that the PATRIOT Act facilitates cooperation between the FBI and CIA, allowing officials to more easily obtain information about individuals suspected to be threats to national security. This allows the two organizations to work together more effectively to thwart criminal activity, including terrorist plots.

PATRIOT Act backers additionally argue that the Act's implementation has proved successful, as there have been no large-scale-terrorist attacks in the United States since September 11. Although the PATRIOT Act does limit some freedoms, its supporters maintain that the Act is essential for our country's betterment and survival. Some enthusiasts also believe that to oppose the PATRIOT Act is to be disloyal to the country.

Arguments Against the PATRIOT Act

Opponents of the PATRIOT Act, such as the American Library Association of Research Libraries, say the legislation undermines the confidentiality that is crucial for the flow of information needed for the provision of library services and, more importantly, for the vitality of our democracy. They contend that people will refrain from obtaining information from some research resources out of fear that each action could lead to trouble.

Other foes of the PATRIOT Act, such as the American Civil Liberties Union and former conservative Republican Congressman Bob Barr, argue that the law threatens rights guaranteed to American citizens in the Fourth Amendment, which states that "the right of the people to be secure in their persons, houses, papers, and effects against unreasonable searches and seizures, shall not be violated; and no warrants shall issue, but upon probable cause, supported by oath or affirmation, and particularly describing the place to be searched and the persons or things to be seized." PATRIOT Act opponents are particularly worried that the Act will encourage the authorities to go on "fishing expeditions" to locate incriminating information from "average citizens."

Bottom Line

To be for the PATRIOT Act does not make one a "patriot" and to be against it does not make one "disloyal." Such labeling merely retards cogent scrutiny of the legislation by solidifying feelings of righteousness and rectitude in one's particular position. A more reasonable approach to study the worth of the Act is to focus on the merits of the arguments made for and against it without resort to name-calling.

Conclusion

American political discourse is rife with over/under-defined terms. Besides the ones discussed, some others include, "the war on terror," "the American people," "bipartisanship," and "family values." To bring such language down to earth requires critical evaluation. Otherwise, we can fool ourselves into thinking we are saying something meaningful when we are just uttering high-level abstractions with no "real" substance.

4

Science Versus Religion: A False Dichotomy

Using historical examples from Western science and Western Christianity, the predominant religion in the Western world, this chapter will investigate the issue of "science versus religion" through the general semantics technique of *dating*. This technique involves attaching dates to our evaluations of people, objects, and situations as a reminder that change occurs over time— for example, John Doe (2006) is not John Doe (2005). Its use can help us to remember that if we want to better understand people, objects, and situations in the present, it makes sense to look back at their past.[1]

"Dating" Science Versus Religion

Science Versus Religion (fourth and fifth century): Faith and Reason

St. Augustine (354–430) was born in North Africa to a Christian mother and a pagan father. He abandoned Christianity because its teachings seemed uncertain or illogical and the Bible seemed full of contradictions and nonsense. After studying Classical philosophers and traveling to Italy, Augustine found an intellectual approach to Christianity (through Neo-Platonism) and biblical exegesis that pleased him, and he eventually was baptized.

St. Augustine argued for four points that not only became fundamental to Christian theology but are key to the science/religion interaction. They are:

- The doctrine of the unity of truth—there is not one truth for theology and another for natural or philosophical knowledge. Contradictions between the two must be resolved intellectually by the use of reason.
- The doctrine of the two books—the Book of Scripture (the Bible) and the Book of Nature (the created world). These are two complementary ways that God reveals himself to humans.
- Scripture and Nature require careful interpretation. For example, biblical passages have layered meanings—a literal, an allegorical, an anagogical, and a moral meaning. Because biblical interpretation is very difficult, our explanations of some passages should be held only provisionally.
- In terms of the pursuit of religion versus the pursuit of science or philosophy, religion has primacy, but scientific knowledge is an important handmaiden that assists true religion.

Science Versus Religion (seventeenth century): The "Galileo Affair"

The "Galileo affair" is an often-cited incident in the history of science religion interactions. Far from being a simple case of science versus religion, it is highly complex and brings up many important philosophical, scientific, and other issues that can best be understood in context.

A key antecedent to the Galileo affair was the publication by Copernicus, in 1543, of his *De revolutionibus orbium coelestium*, which argued that, contrary to the prevailing Ptolemaic-Aristotelian system, the sun was at the center of the universe (heliocentrism) and the Earth revolved around it (geokineticism). For a variety of reasons, his theory found little acceptance.

In 1613, Galileo wrote a letter defending geokineticism and arguing that Scripture had to be interpreted in light of scientific knowledge. He further stated that the biblical story of Joshua's stopping the sun to lengthen the day could be explained thanks to Galileo's discovery of the Sun's rotation, which he suggested, powered the planets. In offering to interpret the Scriptures, Galileo was exceeding his scientific expertise.

In 1615, a Neapolitan priest named Paolo Antonio Forcarini published a book reinterpreting the Bible to be compatible with Copernicanism—this shows that there were clergy on both sides of the issue. He sent a copy to Cardinal Roberto Bellarmino, a highly important theologian, who had given Galileo a verbal warning not to continue to hold Copernicanism as literally true. Bellarmino praised Forcarini and Galileo for speaking "suppositionally and not absolutely," because declaring the absolute truth of the hypotheses would be "dangerous." He also stated that *if* there were an undeniable demonstration of the Earth's motion, then Scripture would have to be reinterpreted very carefully.

But Galileo did not have proof of the earth's motion. His favored "proof"—that the tides are caused by the motion of the earth—was actually incorrect. Although Galileo was ultimately right about heliocentrism, he was wrong to claim he had sound proof of it. Chaos would result if the Bible had to be reinterpreted for every scientific proof.

In 1632–1633, Galileo published a book, *A Dialogue on the*

Two Chief World Systems, which set out arguments for the Ptolemaic and Copernican systems. He put the arguments of Pope Urban VIII on the last page of the book and into the mouth of a fool. The Pope, who was under duress at the time owing to the Thirty Years War and suspicious that Galileo did not reveal to him details of an agreement that he had made with Bellarmino over Copernicanism in 1616, was furious at Galileo for making him look like a simpleton. Galileo was summoned to Rome and questioned. An Inquisition trial was held and Galileo was convicted in June 1633 of "vehement suspicion of heresy." He renounced the Earth's motion and spent the rest of his life under house arrest.

In 1979, Pope John Paul II convened a commission to reinvestigate Galileo's case. Besides an admission of "errors committed" the commission's report contained a reaffirmation of Augustinian principles of exegesis, as upheld by Galileo, and the ultimate compatibility of faith and reason.

Science Versus Religion (eighteenth century): Geology and Biblical Chronology

In the Middle Ages, there was not much reason to think that the Earth and universe were more than a few thousand years old. After all, the Bible was one of the oldest texts known, and there was no alternative evidence to contradict, or significantly supplement its Old Testament chronology.

However, in the seventeenth century, Nicholas Steno, a Danish convert to Catholicism, studied strata and fossils in Tuscany, and he developed geologic theories for their formation. By the end of the seventeenth century, there were attempts to intertwine biblical and geological histories into theories of the earth.

In the eighteenth century, Georges Louis Leclerc Comte De Buffon and Pierre-Simon Laplace proposed new naturalistic theories for origins of the Earth. They progressively increased the age of the Earth, particularly the pre-human period. Such theories were used simultaneously both for and against the reliability of biblical narratives. Some used the findings to reject Genesis entirely, but others saw it as liberating the Bible's spiritual content by emphasizing its meager value for accurate history and chronology.

Theological divisions over how old the earth was revealed a split between elite and popular opinion. A more educated group applied "higher criticism" (the use of standard textual tools to ask questions about authorship, original context, influences, etc.) to the Bible and as a result they were able to accommodate the new scientific geological findings to biblical descriptions. A less educated group rejected such interpretations and insisted on a literal reading of Genesis. This theological split belies the simplistic notion that there is a single religious response to scientific theories.

Science Versus Religion (nineteenth century): Evolution

In 1859, Charles Darwin published his epochal *Origin of Species*. Twelve years later, he published *The Descent of Man*. The scientific and theological rejoinders to these works were complex.

Three important features of Darwin's evolutionary principles were common ancestry, speciation through variation, and natural selection. These ideas impacted theology in diverse ways. For example, there was an impact on biblical authority, specifically in terms of the historicity of Genesis I. Theologians and others who held to strict interpretations of the Bible rejected Darwin's ideas.

The argument for design, an argument for the existence of God based on the belief that there is a design in the visible world, and thus a designer, was eroded by the notion of random variations and natural selection. On an ethical level, the distancing of God and the notion of natural selection—"survival of the fittest"—were seen as undercutting morality in human relations. The origin of man from lower organisms was also considered potentially materialistic. (Materialism is a view that material substance is all that exists—no soul, no spirits, no God. The First Vatican Council explicitly condemned materialism in 1870. In 1950, Pius XII gave conditional support to evolution, and in 1996, John Paul II declared it "more than a hypothesis." However, both popes continued the Church's opposition to materialistic interpretations; the soul exists and is not a product of evolution.) Finally, some theologians found the "lower origins" of man undignified or unsuitable for the *imago Dei*.

Contrary to popular mythology, religious leaders were divided in their reception to Darwinism. A number of religious leaders saw evolution consistent with a divine plan and even as *proof* of the divine purpose of the world. Some found in Darwin support for the biblical teaching that all humankind has a common ancestor (*monogenism*). Liberal theologians, who were anxious to distinguish themselves from conservatives who stuck to biblical literalism, helped to spread evolution. And some conservative theologians, such as the American Baptist minister A. H. Strong argued that humans are no less human even if evolved from beasts. These different responses and reworkings of Darwinian theory by theologians go against facile generalizations concerning the interaction between evolution and Christian thought.

Science Versus Religion (twentieth century): Fundamentalism

By 1900, most American clergy had accommodated some form of an ancient Earth and evolution into their beliefs. The rise of fundamentalism changed this situation.

Fundamentalism as a movement began in the early twentieth century (the name derives from a set of twelve tracts, *The Fundamentals*, published between 1910–1915). It contains an aggregate of beliefs. These include *naïve literalism*, which is a belief that the "surface meaning" of the Bible is literally true; *biblical inerrancy*; and the residuals of nineteenth century millenarist sects—Millenarism gave rise to many apocalyptic beliefs and movements, including the continuing fundamentalist obsession with the New Testament Book of Revelation.

Fundamentalism is as much a social as a religious movement. It is also a reactionary movement in response to social anxiety over the loss of an old order (a religiously oriented Anglo-Saxon Protestant America) and fear of perceived foes (urban culture, modernity, intellectuals, industrialization, and immigration).

Fundamentalist "hot-button" issues have changed over time. Initial opposition was mainly to higher criticism; evolution was treated benignly in *The Fundamentals*. Evolution became a major issue largely in response to the enormous growth of public high schools in the first two decades of the twentieth century that exposed rural populations to modern science.

Fundamentalists gained wide exposure in the famous Scopes "Monkey trial" of 1925. William Jennings Bryan, who had begun crusading against evolution in 1922, was a prosecutor in the case and he was humiliated on the witness stand by defense counsel Clarence Darrow. Due to a legal technicality, the issue of whether states could prohibit the teaching of evolution was not settled in the Scopes case.

Fundamentalist opposition to evolution came back in the 1960s. This return was sparked, in large part, by improved secondary school education in the rural South and Midwest, which included instruction on evolution.

The Creation Research Society, the oldest creation science organization in the United States, was founded in 1963. Creation science is based on naïve literalist readings of Genesis 1 and flood geology—the use of Noah's Flood as an explanation for geological phenomena like mountains, fossils, canyons, etc. In 1968, the Creation Research Society and other supporters of creationism were unsuccessful in stopping the US Supreme Court from overturning a state ban on evolution. After this failure, fundamentalists turned to the *equal-time strategy*. Creation science was promoted as an alternative to evolution.

In 1987, the Supreme Court recognized creation science as religious doctrine, not science. To mask identifiably religious content in order to pass Constitutional muster, *neocreationism*, of which Intelligent Design is a part, was promulgated. Creationists are currently advancing that philosophy as an alternative to evolution.

Although creationists are a minority of the Christian community, their religious views are disproportionately reported on in the media. That is also the case with scientists who espouse "scientism"—a philosophy that exalts the view of science and scientific inquiry to an *absolutely* predominant position, capable of solving, explaining, and/or passing judgment on everything (for some scientism is equivalent to science as religion). Advocates of fundamentalism and advocates of scientism tend to get more news recognition than theologians and scientists who hold more balanced positions because the media favors publicizing controversy and extreme views.

The Big Bang model of the earth's creation, proposed initially in 1927 by Georges Lemaitre, a Belgian priest, offers evidence that science and theological views can "peacefully" coexist. The Big Bang model in its final form upholds the Christian notion of a cosmos with a definite beginning and a *creatio ex nihilo* ("creation out of nothing"). This article of faith stresses that God alone is eternal and is the creator of everything. Pope Pius XII embraced the Big Bang model in 1951.

Science Versus Religion (the present): An Overview

Over the last two hundred years, science and theology have traveled in opposite directions in terms of professionalization, authority, and status. Scientific activity has been regularized by professionalization, granting it greater authority. Theological activity has become diffuse by decreased ability to professionalize theologians, which has resulted in lower-level theology and a loss of status and authority. This trend in theology is exemplified by the triviality of the theological content of the anti-evolution debate (biblical literalism) relative to historical theological positions.

In traditional Christian theology, biblical literalism has been a nonissue. Biblical literalism/evolution may be an issue now because people are not familiar with historical and "high-end" theology. For example, the notion of *secondary causation*—God does not have to directly cause everything. Once God puts things into motion, stuff can happen without divine intervention.

Some scientists, crusading for materialism and atheism, have fanned fundamentalist fears. Such scientists may have forgotten the difference between a *professional* policy of not invoking supernatural action and a *personal credo* against everything supernatural. While it is true that science has furnished theology with a more verifiable sense of man's place in the world (e.g., scientific evidence showing progressive increases in the age of the earth and size of the universe has progressively undercut literalist biblical readings), it is also true that Christian theology has provided significant institutional support (patronage) for studies of the natural world in the last millennium. Moreover, the scholastic tradition of disputation was important to the advancement of science and many founders of modern science were devout religious believers (e.g., Kepler, Copernicus, Galileo, Newton, Boyle).

That theologians and scientists exist in separate camps is a relatively recent division. Movement of ideas between theological and scientific thought has been more usually the case. Historical perspective underscores this fact and can allow us to engage in potentially valuable discourse about science and religion in more thoughtful and productive ways.

PART 2

Sensible Thinking for "Real World" Problems

Practical GS Applications

From the beginning, Korzybski and his students considered general semantics a pragmatic discipline, to be used by individuals, groups, and organizations to solve problems. The first two popular books on the subject, *The Tyranny of Words* by Stuart Chase and *Language in Action* by S. I. Hayakawa (later titled *Language in Thought and Action*) reflected the practical approach as each author used general semantics to examine and assess the influence of language on thought and behavior. Subsequent individuals have employed general semantics to analyze and solve problems in a wide variety of fields including the areas of education, communication, negotiation, management, social science, journalism, and personal adjustment.

Over the years, numerous articles on the benefits of general semantics have appeared in the *General Semantics Bulletin* and *ETC: A Review of General Semantics* and more than 150 doctoral- and master's-degree theses have demonstrated its efficacy. As the following extracts show, general semantics is a highly useful methodology with a wide range of applicability in diverse areas of human endeavor.

General Semantics and . . .

Education
From *General Semantics and the Future of Education* by Rachel Lauer: General semantics has made a great contribution

toward freeing the human race to be fully human. I believe our educational system can and will increasingly use general semantics toward that end because general semantics has features that make it acceptable to educators. It is academic enough for the most bookish scholars, scientific enough for the most critical rationalists, and realistic enough for the most down-to-earth pragmatists.[1]

Teacher Training

From *Introductory Lectures on General Semantics* by Francis P. Chisholm: Training in general semantics is especially important for teachers; it should result in increased efficiency of instruction . . . Among the improvements, which might reasonably be predicated [from learning GS] are:

1. Increased awareness by teachers of "mental" blockages and difficulties in learning by students and improved techniques for removing them.
2. Increased awareness by teachers of the importance of language habits in learning and personality.
3. Better measurement of individual differences.
4. Better understanding of the relationship between subject-matters which are traditionally kept too separate in graduate school training.
5. Better adjustment and understanding of their own (linguistically conditioned) problems by the teachers themselves.[2]

Journalism

From *Journalism Ethics* by John C. Merrill: Journalists work in the field of language; words are the basic tools of their craft. Along with other communicative symbols, such as pictures, words construct the "maps" of the territory of reality. Since language affects thought, and thought affects action, it is easy to see how the meanings we attach to words relate to the field of journalistic ethics. The orientation, called general semantics, expounded by the Polish philosopher, Alfred Korzybski, provides seminal concepts related to words, their meanings, and their implications. An orientation to general semantics will raise the linguistic consciousness of journalists, bring them to a higher level of sophistication, instill in them a recognition of the weakness and the power of words, and generally help them overcome the enslaving tendencies of language.[3]

Psychology

From *Psycho-Logical Fate and Freedom* by Bruce I. Kodish: many major formulators and many practitioners in the related fields of psychotherapy, counseling, and consulting have been influenced by Korzybski. For example, in the area known as "Cognitive-Behavior Therapy," the approach of Rational Emotive Behavior Therapy (REBT) was developed by Albert Ellis, who studied and makes significant use of Korzybski's work. Isabel Caro has developed her Cognitive Therapy of Evaluation based on GS. (Her book, *General Semantics in Psychotherapy*, shows some of the extent of GS influence in that field.) Korzybski's work has also been recognized by Lou Marinoff, one of the leaders in the developing field of "philosophical practice and consulting."[4]

Human Communications

From *Internet webpage comments* by Professor Michael Cole, holder of the Dr. Sanford I. Berman Chair in General Semantics at UCSD: General Semantics is a theory of language and meaning that shares a great deal of methodological and theoretical positions with the contemporary study of human communication. It provides a useful way to come to grips with the new paradigms of human relations and human interaction that have resulted as the forms of communication and mediation between individuals, groups and societies has expanded in the last few centuries. While traditionally considered a critical reflection on the nature of language as a principal medium of human interactions, General Semantics also recognizes that language is inadequate to mediate many new forms of interaction and that, moreover, other kinds of media and tools also regulate the relations of individuals.[5]

Media Ecology

From *Media Ecology is General Semantics Writ Large* by Terence P. Moran: In 1976, when Neil Postman became the editor of *ETC: A Review of General Semantics*, he proposed that the journal expand its areas of concern to include all media of communication. As he liked to say, "Media Ecology is general semantics writ large." When Neil and I started the graduate programs in media ecology at New York University in 1970–71, we based our approaches to understanding media upon the principles of general semantics established by Alfred Korzybski in *Science and Sanity*. We also were influenced by S. I. Hayakawa's *Language in Thought and Action*, Wendell Johnson's *People in Quandaries*, Stuart Chase's *The Tyranny of Words*, the work of Edward Sapir, Benjamin Lee Whorf, and Ludwig Wittgenstein on linguistic relativity, and the work of Adelbert Ames and Hadley Cantril on perception, among others.[6]

Social Work

From *Some Implications of General Semantics Methodology for Social Work* by Eleanor Parkhurst: The study and use of the principles of general semantics can be helpful to the social worker in the development of her personal orientations and adjustment as well as in her treatment of the client[7] . . . the indirect or unwitting application of principles embodied in the system of general semantics may be found in social work theory and practice. It may well be argued that if such 'progress' as has already been made in the field of social work is based on the unconscious use of these principles, still further 'progress' may be hastened and made to touch on more aspects of that field by the direct and continuous application of this general methodology.[8]

Business Management

From *Managerial Judgment and Critical Thinking* by William Exton Jr.: As a management consultant, I searched for a consistent integrated methodology—one which was so general in its applicability that it would be taught *per se,* or in relation to virtually any other body content. I wanted an intellectual discipline—at least potentially rigorous—which provided synergistic formulations with a history of successful applications. Fortunately, such a discipline already existed, known internationally as general semantics.[9]

Industrial Engineering

From *General Semantics for Engineers?!* by Wilson J. Bentley: A one-credit hour course has been conducted at Oklahoma State University since the spring of 1955. The course is required of all third-year industrial engineering students in the undergraduate School of Industrial Engineering and

56

Management.[10] . . . As the instructor of this course I do not deceive myself into believing that I am instrumental in completely changing the life and character of these industrial engineers. But I'm pleased many alumni say this is the *one* course they remember. It appears that each student feels he got at least one good idea from the text and discussion. Good ideas are scarce. The experiment has been successful. So I plan to continue to talk to engineers about general semantics.[11]

Technical Assistance Work

From *General Semantics in Technical Assistance Work* by Sixten E. Flach: A man or woman from what we call the Western World who takes an assignment as a United Nations technical assistance adviser to an underdeveloped country must be prepared to meet problems different from those he usually meets in his own country. In my experience, the adviser should not only be thoroughly informed about the general conditions—particularly the cultural conditions—of the country to which he is assigned, but he should also be familiar with the principles of general semantics. I am thinking of general semantics here as a scientific orientation or attitude—what Wendell Johnson called "a systematic attempt to formulate the general method of science in such a way that is might be applied not only in a few restricted areas of human experience, but *generally* in daily life."[12]

Psychiatry

From *General Semantics, Psychiatry, Psychotherapy and Prevention* by Alfred Korzybski: Although general semantics is not a medical science, it has been a help to psychiatrists in dealing with their patients. I refer, of course, to psychiatrists

who have gone through training in general semantics.
General practitioners have also found general semantics very
helpful.[13]

Negotiation

From *The Complete Negotiator* by Gerard I. Nierenberg: I
have searched for the vital ethical center, that negotiators can
relate to. It is time-binding . . . In "General Semantics and
Human Values," *General Semantics Bulletin*, Winter-Spring,
(1952), Dr. J. S. A. Bois reported: "Our course has become a
full program of study and application of 'G.S. Methods for
Executives,' and it has been used in varying degrees by
individuals or groups of executives" . . . "They generally
report that it makes them 'better men,' more willing to 'give
and take' etc. Some eventually discover 'that G.S. gives a
scientific foundation to the Golden Rule.'"[14]

The Law

From *How Just is Our System of Justice?* by Frank Scardilli:
Research shows that it is an article of faith among most
Americans, including our judges and lawyers, that the US
has the best system of justice in the world. Two obvious
general semantics questions are: What do you mean? and
How do you know? To the extent some may be using the
terms "law" and "justice" interchangeably some caveats are in
order . . . Some of our most prominent jurists have been
highly critical of our overly adversarial legal system dating as
far back as the Eisenhower Era when Chief Justice Earl
Warren predicted its early demise. Perhaps its survival
reflects the feisty rugged individualism, which has
historically served Americans well but may require serious
reexamination in today's interdependent world where the

vast majority of the nations reject our adversarial legal model. Moreover, we should not ignore the impact of its high cost on the quality and quantity of justice available in a society where experts say there is too much law for those who can afford it but not enough for those who cannot . . . In my opinion, a re-evaluation of the pros and cons of the adversarial system using the tools of general semantics would be most instructive in shedding further light on whether that system needs to be changed.[15]

Investing

From *The General Semantics of Wall Street* by John Magee: Wall Street, as we use the word, is an abstraction, a symbol. It is real enough, but it isn't the kind of reality that you can go and look at, and take pictures of, and walk around. It is a metaphor . . . To understand the strange and often irrational things that people do to themselves in Wall Street, it is necessary to explore the forces that operate on them, largely from within themselves. And, when you have traced these relations and understand them [using general semantics] at the levels of high abstraction, you may find when you come down to earth again that some of the puzzling and threatening problems of the market, and of life in all its other aspects, do not seem so puzzling and so threatening as they used to seem.[16]

Teaching Writing in College

From *Building Critical Thinking Into a Freshman Writing Course* by Linda Anstendig: Thinking about critical thinking and general semantics, first in Dr. Rachel Lauer's faculty development workshop at Pace University, and then in my classroom applications, has led me to make significant changes in my teaching. Content and methodology have begun to mesh more closely as I have redesigned my Freshman Developmental Writing course, trying to provide my students with conceptual tools and the ability to better analyze the materials of any discipline.[17]

Teaching Physics

From *General Semantics and the Teaching of Physics* by Alvin M. Weinberg: The particular system of semantics which appears to me to me most useful in coping with certain problems in the teaching of physics is the one formulated by Alfred Korzybski in his remarkable book, *Science and Sanity*. This original work is necessarily repetitious in its presentation—it was addressed primarily to psychiatrists not laymen but there is such a wealth of pertinent material throughout the volume that the patient reader will be amazed by the wide applicability of the materials outlined in it.[18]

Organizational Leadership

From *Using GS to Enhance Organizational Leadership* by Martin H. Levinson: Can we use general semantics to enhance organizational leadership? In my experience, more than fifteen years as an educational administrator in the New York City school system, it certainly can[19] . . . To become a transformational leader, I recommend the use of GS ideas and formulations. They clearly helped me to improve my program.[20]

Philosophy

From *General Semantics Guides Toward Better Futures* by Milton Dawes: I start with quotes from two philosophers:

One from Bernard Lonergan, S.J., and the other from William James. Bernard Lonergan, S.J., wrote this about method. "A method is a set of directives that serve to guide a process toward a result." William James wrote: "Philosophy is an unreasonably stubborn effort to think clearly." We can apply these two time-binding gems to general semantics in this manner: general semantics provides us with a set of time-binding directives that we can use as guides to clarify our thinking and help us create better futures.[21]

Interdisciplinary Studies

From *What Do You Mean and How Do You Know?* by Nicholas Johnson: General semantics draws upon, and contributes to, many academic fields of study. Indeed, one of general semantics' great strengths over the years has been the near universal professional and academic applicability of the insights it makes possible.[22]

Anthropology

From Bronislaw Malinowski's testimonial in *Science and Sanity*: The functional or relational conception of matter, mind and, finally, of human culture, seems to be generally crystallizing from all attempts at scientific synthesis. Count Korzybski's work contributes to those efforts in no mean measure.[23]

The Social Sciences

From *General Semantics and the Social Sciences* by William J. Williams: We, in the social sciences, public administration, and education in general, are being requested to supply those who look to us with a meaning for life. It throws us immediately and directly into the depths of psychological, philosophical and epistemological concerns . . . The General Semantics epistemological process provides us with the opportunity [to deal with such concerns]. Thus, the reasons for adopting this methodology.[24]

Creative Thinking

From *For the Newcomer to General Semantics* by Mary Morain: By simplifying much that is complex, general semantics has helped thousands of individuals to better understand themselves, other people, and their environment. Personal relations are improved as communication blockages are dissolved. Considerable freedom rises when the rigidity of language ceases to control thinking and responses. Pressures formerly producing stress are often lessened. Debilitating automatic responses and self-defeating tendencies to jump to conclusions become less frequent. It is commonplace to experience a sense of renewed personal well-being and creative release. Outworn ideas can more easily be shed, leaving the mind open to fresh observations, more creative thinking.[25]

Child Rearing

From *Bringing Up the Family Semantically* by Alice P. Cherbeneau: We have been trying to teach our children the process of abstraction to aid them in avoiding identification and allness reactions. Korzybski's chapter on "Non-Aristotelian Training" in *Science and Sanity* has some very interesting suggestions. We have used the apple, the orange, and other objects to demonstrate the abstracting process and to illustrate the changing in-process nature of our world. I agree with [general semantics expert] Dr. Irving Lee that, "Our language use too often emphasizes the static. We speak as if life facts were not changing, as if our statements fit for 'all-time.' The time factor must become a part of human orientation."[26]

Critical Thinking

From Steve Allen's "Foreword" in *Thinking Creatically*: I shall never forget the literal thrill I felt some years ago at witnessing a demonstration by a group of children aged 12 or 13, all of whom had benefited from instruction in general semantics by Catherine Minteer. Each child first read aloud a newspaper article or advertisement, then analyzed it for the audience. The insight, the clarity, the brilliance with which those children separated hot air from factual, reasonable statements was tremendously exciting. God, if a generation of young Americans could be taught similar lessons, it is difficult to envision the benefits to society that could result.[27]

The Prevention of Bullying

From *A General Semantics Approach to School-Age Bullying* by Katherine Liepe-Levinson and Martin H. Levinson: During the past fifty years numerous studies have demonstrated that general semantics instruction has positive effects on student attitudes, behavior, and learning. These effects include increased critical thinking, enhanced creativity, improved composition writing, improved personality adjustment, decreased prejudice, and decreased alienation. The positive feedback that we have received from students, teachers, and parents on our bully prevention workshops indicate that this is yet another area where general semantics training has proven beneficial in an educational setting.[28]

Self-Help

From *Levels of Knowing and Existence* by Harry L. Weinberg: General semantics is a rational [self-help] methodology to be used by the individual himself[29] . . . General semantics is not a panacea; it will not end all anxieties, alleviate all worries, give *the* answer to the infinite varieties of complexities that all of us face. Rather, it is an aid, a potent one, among other tools man has developed for controlling both his external and internal environments.[30]

Problem Solving

From *Drive Yourself Sane* by Susan Presby Kodish and Bruce I. Kodish: While we don't view general semantics as a substitute for therapy, using it can create broad therapeutic effects in helping you to solve problems and communicate well. Preventively, using it can help you to avoid problems and create greater opportunities. Many people apply it to their professional lives, as well as it use to improve their day-to-day activities and relationships. Teachers, health professionals, psychologists, business people, engineers, computer specialists, artists, lawyers and other find it of great value in helping to resolve individual, organizational and global problems. [31]

Human Evaluating

From *Korzybski and Semantics* by Stuart Chase: I can testify that twenty years of exposure to General Semantics have demonstrated that the evaluation of men and events can be sharpened by its use, that certain mental blocks can be remedied, that one's writing can be clarified. Students of General Semantics report a better ability to listen, a reduction in the terrors of stage fright, help in cases of stuttering. General Semantics can aid in teaching children to understand their world, and in bringing "backward" scholars up to mark. It has led to a healthy re-examination of verbal proof.[32]

Ethics

From *Time-Binding: To Build a Fire* by James D. French: For the society that adopts it, Korzybski's theory could provide a secure, rational foundation for ethical behavior, an ethics based on the verifiable facts of human interdependence in time and space. If taught well in the schools, the theory could transform the whole outlook of our culture. Because time-binding is fully compatible with the great religions and science, it can be the foundation of a new American ethic.[33]

Emotional Intelligence

From *General Semantics and Emotional Intelligence* by Martin H. Levinson: Since its inception, general semantics has been quite involved with "emotional intelligence." *Science and Sanity* (1933), the book that launched GS, focused heavily on how to increase human cooperation and reduce human misery and Wendell Johnson's GS classic, *People in Quandaries* (1946), had as its subtitle *The Semantics of Personal Adjustment.* S. I. Hayakawa named his book *Language in Action* (1941) and Irving J. Lee wrote texts titled *Language Habits in Human Affairs* (1941) and *The Language of Wisdom and Folly* (1949). In the 1950s, J. Samuel Bois' concern with emotion was evident in the title he chose for his book, *Explorations in Awareness* (1957). Today the tradition continues, with GS volumes such as *Developing Sanity in Human Affairs* (1998) and *Drive Yourself Sane*

(2001); with IGS seminars that deal with educating people on the complex nature and inter-relatedness of thoughts and feelings; and with chapters in using general semantics in emotional self-management in *Sensible Thinking for Turbulent Times* (2006).[34]

The Art of Listening

From *Do You Know How to Listen?* by Wendell Johnson: Another significant contribution to the art of listening has been made in recent years by general semantics. General semantics is by no means exclusively concerned with the art of listening. It provides a general approach to problems of evaluation, stressing the rudiments of the scientific method, so formulated as to be useful moment to moment in daily living. The contributions it makes to the art of listening are to be found especially in certain key questions it encourages the listener to ponder as he attends to any speaker.[35]

Intercultural Communication

From *General Semantics and Intercultural Communication* by Mitsuko Saito-Fukunaga: In dealing with members of another culture, "extensional" [general semantics] devices can be used to help enable the listener to distinguish and react to nonverbal realities instead of verbal expressions. The five such devices briefly mentioned below are useful aids in keeping our minds open when listening and speaking . . . Using these devices will help improve mutual understanding in intercultural communication.[36]

Feminism(s)

From *Glossing Over Feminism: A General Semantics Critique* by Katherine Liepe-Levinson and Martin H. Levinson: It makes sense that the term "feminism" would find its way into an array of glossaries, because the function of a glossary, in general, is to define and clarify terms. In our culture the word "feminism" covers enough ideological, intellectual, practical, and sensational territory to stir any number of map-makers into action. [The General Semantics glossary of Robert Pula] would appear to be an excellent forum to explore the diverse philosophic systems that make up the territory of "feminisms."[37]

Semiotics

From *General Semantics and Semiotics* by Andrew Lohrey: Semiotic analysis has traditionally been seen as the study of signs. Ever since Ferdinand de Saussure first proposed the science early this century there has been a growing interest in the subject. (1) It is doubtful if Alfred Korzybski ever read Saussure but much of the general semantics approach to language corresponds with semiotic analysis. (2) There are of course many differences, yet the differences seem to me to be ones that are mutually strengthening. What do I mean by this? Well, in regard to semiotics, in that area which has traditionally generated most controversy, that is, in the exclusion of a physical referent from the sign structure, I see Korzybski's work as providing some answers.[38]

Neurolinguistic Programming

From *Korzybski and General Semantics* by George Doris: Korzybski spoke of '*neuro-semantic*' and '*neuro-linguistic*' reactions—holistic terms for the functioning of the 'human-organism-as-a-whole-in-an-environment', with hyphens deliberately used to indicate interconnectedness. Readers of this magazine may now recognize a link with Neurolinguistic

Programming, a recent development described in *The Structure of Magic, I and II*—books about language, therapy, communication and change. The authors, John Grinder, a linguist, and Richard Bandler, a gestalt therapist—indicate their familiarity with Korzybski's formulations by quoting him and citing *Science and Sanity*. The two 'wizards' they cite by name, Virginia Satir and Fritz Perls, have [also] acknowledged a debt to Korzybski. [39]

Self-Management
From *Management of Stress* by Milton Dawes: In short, general semantics addresses the dynamics and structure of our intrapersonal, interpersonal, and inter-environmental communications, interactions, interrelationships, and as such is relevant to the understanding, orientation, and effective management of ourselves in our semantic environments. [40]

Science Fiction
From *GS/SF* by Jeremy Klein: The tangled relation of general semantics to science fiction began within seven years of the publication of *Science and Sanity*. John W. Campbell, Jr., the influential editor of *Astounding Science Fiction* magazine, who regarded general semantics as a prototype "future science" encouraged several of his most popular writers to familiarize themselves with the general semantics literature. Campbell hoped they would incorporate some general semantics theory or methodology in their stories. Several writers did so, most notably A. E. van Vogt in his "null-A" novels, and Robert Heinlein, whose standard protagonist, the "competent man," embodied the evaluative and reasoning habits encouraged by general semantics authors and instructors. General semantics figured in other

ways too—as an indirect target of William Tenn's satire in his short story "Null P" and as a source of new words (see, for example, Philip K. Dick's idiosyncratic use of the term "time-binding" in his novel *Flow My Tears, the Policeman Said*).[41]

Design

From *An Approach to Design* by Norman T. Newton: So long as we remain human we are going to continue using languages for communication, be it about design or about any other aspect of human living . . . [And] we can at least try to be aware of the structural implications of our thought and of the language, in which we express it . . . An admirable, extensive, yet simple treatment of that topic will be found in the works of Lee, Johnson, Hayakawa, and others. A careful study of these accounts will surely give you a keener insight into the entire question of verbal structure as compared with visual structure, especially in the realm of human use of symbol systems.[42]

The Efficient Use of Human Energy

From *The Management of Time* by James T. McCay: Back in the 1920s, a Polish mathematician, engineer, and student of human behavior, Count Alfred Korzybski, worked out a theory of control at the level of the elements of our experience. He spent the rest of his life trying to help people recognize the value of his discovery. Later, Dr. J. S. Bois developed an observing grid based on Korzybski's theory. He tested it and found that it yielded results beyond his expectations . . . [It was] a grid for discovering energy losses in time to prevent them from taking place.[43]

Art Appreciation

From *General Semantics and Modern Art* by Oliver Bloodstein: Korzybski's method of general re-training of semantic reactions is particularly well adapted to orientational requirements for the 'comprehension' of modern art. He says, "We can train appropriate reactions simply and effectively by 'silence on the objective levels,' using familiar objects called 'a chair,' or 'a pencil,' and this training automatically affects our 'emotions,' 'feelings,' as well as other psycho-logical immediate responses difficult to reach, which are also not words." Training of this kind is precisely what is required to facilitate lower order response to the structural meaning of modern art.[44]

Poetry

From *Poetry Ring* by Lance Strate and Dale Winslow: Given his emphasis on scientific method and rationality, it would be easy to assume that Korzybski only valued the languages of science and mathematics, and had no room for the arts. But quite to the contrary, he had great appreciation for the arts; in fact, he was married to the noted American painter, Mira Edgerly; and as for poetry, he wrote the following in *Science and Sanity* as part of his discussion on multiordinality:

In a certain sense, such a use of *m.o.* terms is to be found in poetry, and it is well known that many scientists, particularly the creative ones, like poetry. Moreover, poetry conveys in a few sentences more of lasting value than a whole volume of scientific analysis. The free use of *m.o.* terms without the bother of a structurally impossible formalism outside of mathematics accomplishes this, *provided we are conscious of abstracting; otherwise only confusion results.*[45]

6

General Semantics and
Rational Emotive Behavior Therapy

Rational-Emotive Behavior Therapy (REBT), Albert Ellis's internationally renowned theory of human adjustment, is largely based on three foundational pillars: wisdom from the Roman Stoic Philosopher Epictetus ("People are not disturbed by things but by the view they take of them"), insights from the psychoanalyst Karen Horney ("the tyranny of the shoulds"), and formulations from Alfred Korybski, the founder of general semantics (a science-based "self-help" system aimed at helping individuals and groups make more intelligent decisions). This chapter will focus on the last pillar and show how formulations of general semantics (GS) and insights from REBT can undercut irrational human thinking.

The ABCs of REBT

According to Ellis's "ABCs," our emotional and behavioral reactions are the result of the following sequence:

A) We first experience an Activating Event (e.g., someone calls us a "bad" name).

B) We have Beliefs or Thoughts about that Event (that person should not say things like that—it's terrible that person called me a name—how embarrassing!).

C) We experience the Emotional Consequences of our beliefs and thoughts (I hate that person! I feel depressed/angry/scared! I want to crawl into a hole! I want to get back at that person!), which often leads to Behavioral Consequences (withdrawal, fighting, crying, etc.).

To keep from having to endure the negative effects of dysfunctional emotional and behavioral Cs (Consequences), REBT suggests we examine our Bs (Beliefs or thoughts) and replace those that are irrational with rational ones. What follows are REBT and GS ideas that can help us to do that. (The ten irrational beliefs appearing on the subsequent pages come from *A New Guide to Rational Living* by Albert Ellis.)

Ten Irrational Beliefs with REBT and GS Correctives

Irrational Belief # 1: You must have love or approval from all the people you find significant.

What makes this belief irrational is the *must* that accompanies it. It is rational to prefer that people give you love and approval, but REBT theory would point out that demanding they do is illogical because in most life situations you cannot force others to behave the way you want them to.

Some may argue that receiving love and approval is a basic necessity for human existence and happiness. But the fact is, throughout history there have been people who have lived in solitude without dying or feeling terribly unhappy, and there have been people who have lived in social groups without getting upset that others do not like them. Obviously there are *some* individuals who do not *need* acceptance. *Some* individuals do not even *want* love.

But most of us *prefer* or *desire* acceptance and feel happier with some measure of approval. Such wants and longings are rational preferences. The GS notion of *indexing* can help us to counter negative and inaccurate self-talk relating to such preferences.

Indexing is a general semantics tool that involves using numerical designations to examine cases within a larger category. Its use can help us to find differences that might make a difference. For example, an individual may complain that *nobody* likes him. However, using the indexing tool, this mortal may come to realize that although persons one, two, and three do not "sing his praises," that is not the case with person number four, who has steered several complimentary remarks in his direction. Indexing people, places, and things can assist individuals to see "reality" more clearly and to make more accurate inferences and generalizations about what is going on.

Irrational Belief # 2: You must be thoroughly competent, adequate, and achieving.

Like the previous irrational thought, it is the *must* that makes this belief irrational. Preferring that you perform in a thoroughly competent, adequate, and achieving manner is rational. But demanding that you do is illogical because it is impossible for a person to *always* function at 100 percent capacity and to have conditions *always* be conducive to one's best efforts.

The irrational demand to do well in everything one tries can result in depression or anger if one does less than well in a particular activity. A more rational conception is that "doing" is more important than "doing well." G. K. Chesterton went so far as to say, "If a thing is worth doing, it is worth doing badly."

People have many skills and abilities. Success does not make an individual worthy and failure does not make an individual worthless. It is far more rational to accept oneself as intrinsically valuable and meritorious than to link one's value with one's achievements. People are far too complex to be given ratings, or to rate themselves, on all aspects of their life. Who would decide which aspects are the most meaningful? Are verbal skills more important than mechanical skills?

It is true that one can "objectively" measure failure in an activity—for example, you receive 40 percent on an English exam or a tennis match is lost. But when you define yourself as "a failure" you are engaging in what philosopher Bertrand Russell calls a "category error." For the things you are failing at are in one category and you, the doer of those things, are in quite a different category. We all have various levels of mastery in the projects we undertake. So if we categorize our performance in these projects as "successes" or "failures," we jump to a different category when we call ourselves, the doers, "successes" or "failures." We are not what we do. Consequently, it is sensible to rate only the things we do and not identify them with who we are, which is quite a different category.

Wendell Johnson, in his GS classic *People in Quandaries*, states that people who demand that they must do well can end up with a case of *IFD disease*. This malady describes a condition in which high ideals combined with continued frustration can lead a person to become demoralized (IFD specifically refers to an individual going from Idealization to Frustration to Demoralization). People who become demoralized sometimes get angry with themselves or others for causing this problem.

Setting realistic goals is an excellent strategy for preventing IFD disease. In addition, it is helpful to underscore the notion that failure to reach one's goals does not mean that *you* are a failure. Defining oneself that way is factually incorrect and self-defeating.

Irrational Belief # 3: When people act obnoxiously and unfairly you should blame and damn them and see them as bad, wicked, or rotten individuals.

Blaming people confuses their wrongful *acts* with their sinful *essence*. But no matter how many "evil acts" a person performs, *they* cannot remain intrinsically evil because they could in the future change their behavior and commit no additional wrongdoings. Furthermore, if one cares to look, one can find that "bad" people do occasionally perform "good" acts. That is so because human beings function, to use GS parlance, as *organisms-as-wholes-in-environments*. (According to this GS formulation, individuals are complex entities who behave differently in diverse settings and circumstances.)

Blaming others typically leads people to become angry and exhibit other manifestations of hostility such as high blood pressure and stomach distress. Such irritability deflects attention from coming up with ways to effectively induce the "blamee" to behave in a manner more to our liking. Moreover, reflexively responding with anger to the actions of others gives control of our emotions over to them.

REBT maintains, along with Epictetus, that "People are not disturbed by things, but by the views they take of them." In other words, feelings are based on thoughts. That means we have power over our emotions. The irrational belief that other people make us angry lets them be the arbiters of our emotional well-being. In doing this we set ourselves up as targets for emotional button-pushers.

To keep from becoming such a target, general semantics recommends delaying one's reactions and giving some thought to what is going on in a particular circumstance before responding to what are perceived as slights and affronts. Typically, the use of the *delayed reaction* technique, which involves the human ability to consciously engage one's higher brain functions and delay long enough to evaluate something before reacting to it, produces much more effective responses in situations than reacting impulsively by cursing and damning others for their insulting remarks or behavior.

Irrational Belief # 4: You must view things as terrible, awful, and horrible when you get seriously frustrated, treated unfairly, or rejected.

"Musterbation" is at work here. We do not *have to* become miserable and depressed if we are seriously frustrated, treated unfairly, or rejected. As rational creatures, we can choose to view "toxic" situations in less noxious ways. For example, let's say that you have been dating someone for a long time and that individual breaks up with you. Do you have to sink into despair? Not if you're a general semanticist.

Students of GS know from science that at each moment everything in the world is changing, sometimes slowly and sometimes very quickly. Because things are constantly in flux, general semantics suggests that to get good results in circumstances it is important to adapt in order to respond appropriately. One appropriate response in the aforementioned dating situation would be to make plans to start dating again. As the cliché goes, there are many fish in the sea.

You can cause yourself to suffer if you pick out a negative detail in a situation and dwell on it exclusively, thus perceiving the whole situation as negative. The technical name for this process is *selective abstraction*, a bad habit that can cause one to suffer needless anguish. To overcome this habit one can follow the advice of general semantics to be more conscious of how one "abstracts."

For example, an executive I knew by the name of Bill had a boss who was micromanaging a project that he had asked Bill to put together. Bill resented his boss's interference because it was slowing down the work. The boss was also acting rudely to Bill, who eventually became quite depressed about the whole situation.

I suggested to Bill that he was only concentrating on the negative aspects of the problem. I advised he take a more balanced view of what was going on and think about the positive input he was getting from his clients and colleagues on his work. I also asked Bill to review the notion that his boss might be jealous that Bill was getting accolades from others for the project. Bill considered my counsel, went beyond his negative thinking, and his mood improved. Seeing his situation more expansively had boosted his frame of mind.

Irrational Belief # 5: Emotional misery comes from external pressures, and you have little ability to control or change your feelings.

REBT emphasizes that outside people and events can do nothing, at worst, but harm you physically or cause you various kinds of discomfort or deprivation. Most of the pain other people "cause" you (especially feelings of horror, panic, shame, guilt, and hostility) actually stems from your taking their reactions too seriously; by your falsely telling yourself that you cannot stand their disapproval or enjoy life without their acceptance.

General semantics stresses that you can have power over your reactions to words. For example, if someone calls you "stupid," rather than speedily replying with an insult of your own you can analyze the situation. Does being called stupid actually make you stupid? Can a mere word magically change someone into something a person is not? Is it smart to let another individual control your reactions through being called a name? These questions suggest that outside influences are only influences and that you can be the "captain of your ship, the master of your soul."

General semantics also notes that when we say and believe that we detest, hate, or can't stand something, we become more upset than if we merely disliked the thing. Overreacting to situations can lead one to become angry and distraught. Thinking more objectively (general semantics calls such thinking *extensional*) can prevent such dysfunctional emoting.

To wit, a businessman I know named Tom hated going to Monday morning meetings. Precious little got done at these weekly confabs and, to add insult to injury, he had to endure his colleagues' posturing and "kissing up" to the boss. Sunday nights were miserable for Tom because he knew the following day he would have to attend the dreaded Monday morning meeting.

To help Tom to overcome his overreactions to Monday morning meetings, I suggested that he ask himself the following *extensional* questions: "Can I really not stand these meetings, or do I really mean that I do not like them?" "Is my overreacting helping me or making things worse?" "Where is it written that everything at work should be pleasant and delightful for me?" Tom thought hard about these questions and came to realize that, while attending Monday morning meetings was not a top ten experience for him, it was not the hell he was making it out to be. Changing his thinking had changed his outlook on the situation.

Irrational Belief # 6: If something seems dangerous or fearsome, you must preoccupy yourself with and make yourself anxious about it.

REBT gives emphasis to the notion that if something seems truly dangerous or fearsome, you may take two intelligent approaches: determine whether this thing *actually* involves danger or (if you can do nothing) resign yourself to the fact of its existence. Becoming anxious (i.e., exhibiting overconcern or exaggerated fear) about it or continually reiterating the horror of a potentially or actually fearsome situation will not change it or better prepare you to cope with it. On the contrary, the more you upset yourself, the less able you will prove, in almost all instances, to accurately assess and cope with this danger.

General semantics suggests using *probability thinking* to help beat anxiety. Such thinking can help combat an anxious person's "what-ifs." ("What if my company downsizes!" "What if the boss hates my report!" "What if I don't meet my sales quota this month!" The person who says "what-if" takes a situation or event that *could* happen and makes it something that probably *will* happen.)

I explained the idea of probability thinking to a friend of mine, who made the "what-if" statements in the previous paragraph, and he decided to use it to allay his anxiety. To his three "what-if" assertions, he responded: "If my company downsizes there is a strong possibility that nothing will happen to me since I have fifteen years of seniority in my position." "If my boss hates my report he will probably criticize me for it and ask me to do another one. I can live with that." "If I don't meet my sales quota this month I will make less money than I did last month. But chances are good that there won't be any other repercussions." Probability thinking is a useful antidote to "what-if-itis."

Irrational Belief # 7: You can more easily avoid facing life difficulties and self-responsibilities than undertake rewarding forms of self-discipline.

Practitioners of this philosophy tend to accomplish very little in life because most high-level accomplishments (e.g., writing a novel, maintaining a long-term relationship, learning a foreign language) require perseverance and self-discipline. Avoidance of life and self-responsibilities leads, in most instances, to less satisfying activities and less confidence.

REBT notes that in avoiding certain difficulties of life we almost always tend to exaggerate their pain and discomfort. For example, a person may think they won't be able to stand the pain at the dentist's office or they will faint if they undertake a public speaking engagement. When people think this way they are confusing their inferences with facts (the vast majority of people are able to handle the pain at the dentist's office and an exceedingly small percentage of people faint when making speeches).

To make accurate assessments of situations, and to avoid jumping to wrong conclusions about them, it is useful to know how to distinguish facts from inferences. Unfortunately, the ability to do this, an aptitude that is highly emphasized in general semantics, is often poorly developed in people (one reason for this is that fact/inference discrimination is not stressed enough in school).

Individuals who bring exaggerated fears to life difficulties could benefit greatly by learning how to distinguish the difference between facts and inferences. Some of these differences include the following: Statements of fact are made after observation of experience, are confined to what one observes or experiences, and represent a high degree of probability. Statements of inference are made anytime—before, during, or after observation, go beyond what one observes or experiences, and represent some degree of probability.

Since we must make inferences it is important to make accurate ones. To do that, general semantics suggests that we take into consideration the variety of possible causes of an event and the variety of reactions we are capable of. Additionally, to be more confident of our inferences, GS counsels that we base them on observations and that they converge—a number of inferences point to the same conclusion.

Irrational Belief # 8: Your past remains all-important and because something once strongly influenced your life it has to keep determining your feelings and behavior today.

REBT underscores that a strong belief in the enormous significance of the past proves irrational for several reasons: (a) it promotes illogical overgeneralizations (e.g., because you once felt too weak to stand up against the dominance of your mother hardly means that you must *always* remain that weak); (b) by allowing yourself to remain too strongly influenced by past events, you cease to look for alternative solutions to problems; (c) behaviors that worked in childhood will not necessarily work in adulthood (e.g., children wail, balk, and throw tantrums to get their way with parents but adults who use these behaviors with other adults are unlikely to have similar success).

The Greek philosopher Heraclitus maintained over two thousand years ago that one cannot step twice in the same river. Science has confirmed this process view of existence and has demonstrated that everything in the world is constantly changing. That includes people.

Individuals change over time as new facts present themselves and new circumstances emerge. Are you the same person today that you were a year ago, five years ago, ten years ago? Do you look exactly identical? Has your behavior remained exactly the same? The world and people in it vary over time. Life is process, so change must occur.

Dating (a GS tool that involves attaching dates to our evaluations of people, ideas, and things) can help us stay attuned to the fact that we live in a changing world. For example, Joe (who is working out this month) is not Joe (sans workout, last month), technology (2012) is not technology (2002), American-made cars (today) are not American-made cars (manufactured in the 1950s). And you (currently) are not you (in bygone days). This last actuality can help a person to overcome the irrational belief that the past must remain all-important in determining one's feelings and behavior in the present.

Irrational Belief # 9: People and things should turn out better than they do and that you must view it as awful and horrible if you do not find good solutions to life's grim realities.

REBT makes clear that this is an idiotic idea for several reasons:

- Although you might find it lovely if things and events did *not* occur the way they do, they frequently *will.*
- When people behave other than the way you like, they usually do not affect you too perniciously unless you *think* they do.
- Upsetting yourself about other people and events will usually sidetrack you from your logical main concern: the way *you* behave, the things *you* do.
- The notion that an absolutely perfect solution to any of life's problems exists has little probability since few

things remain all black or all white, and normally many alternative solutions prove viable.

With respect to this last point, as there are no perfect solutions to life's difficulties, it makes sense to accept compromises and *reasonable* answers. To come up with such answers, general semantics recommends the use of the scientific method: (a) attempt objectively to see various sides of the issue with a minimum of prejudices and preconceptions; (b) choose a solution and try it out experimentally—understanding that it may work out well, and it may not; (c) evaluate the results and revise your approach if necessary.

The scientific method has made possible the wonders of modern medicine and modern technology. Alfred Korzybski and other practitioners of general semantics have shown since 1933, when *Science and Sanity* was first published, that the scientific method can be just as effective for solving problems of everyday living.

Irrational Belief # 10: You can achieve maximum human happiness by inertia and inaction or by passively and "uncommittedly" enjoying yourself."

REBT points out that this notion is irrational for a number of reasons:

1. Humans rarely feel particularly happy or alive when inert, except for short periods of time between exertions.
2. Most "intelligent and perceptive people" seem to require vitally absorbing activity to stay maximally alive and happy.

3. To some degree, human contentment seems almost synonymous with absorption in outside people and events, what psychologist Nina Bull calls "goal orientation."
4. Work confidence seems intrinsically related to activity.
5. Inertia has a tendency to perniciously accumulate.

Alfred Korzybski recognized that the linchpin for optimal human happiness is setting realistic goals and persevering toward achieving them. In general semantics that recognition is labeled the *extensional theory of happiness*. It has been my experience that those who practice this theory tend to be happier and more productive than those who don't.

7

General Semantics and
Emotional Intelligence

In 1995, Daniel Goleman, a science reporter for the *New York Times*, published the international bestseller *Emotional Intelligence: Why it Can Matter More than IQ*. The impetus for the book was an article he chanced upon in a small academic journal by two psychologists, John D. Mayer and Peter Salovey. Their piece, published in 1990, contained the first formulation of a concept they labeled *emotional intelligence*.[1]

These days the phrase emotional intelligence is ubiquitous, showing up in the cartoon strips *Dilbert* and *Zippy the Pinhead*, in Roz Chast's sequential art in *The New Yorker*, in "Social and Emotional Learning" (SEL) programs, and in professional development workshops.[2] *Harvard Business Review* calls "EI" a "ground-breaking, paradigm-shattering idea, one of the most influential business notions in a decade."[3]

This chapter will examine some of the key biological and theoretical underpinnings that support the concept of emotional intelligence. In addition, it will show how the tools and formulations of general semantics (GS) can help a person to attain mastery in an area that is, according to Goleman, redefining what it means to be "smart"—research indicates that IQ accounts for only about 20 percent of career success.[4]

Emotions and the Brain

Folk wisdom uses the expressions "heart" and "head" to express the difference between "feelings" and "rational thinking" ("I know it in my heart" is different than, and usually more powerful, than knowing through reason).[5] The emotion/thought dichotomy is sometimes also conceived in terms of an "emotional brain" and a "reasoning brain." Commenting on the two-part division of reason and emotion, the sixteenth-century humanist Erasmus of Rotterdam said:

"Jupiter has bestowed far more passion than reason—you could calculate the ratio as 24 to one. He set up two raging tyrants to Reason's solitary power: anger and lust. How far Reason can prevail against the combined forces of these two the common life of man makes quite clear. Reason does the only thing she can and shouts herself hoarse, repeating formulas of virtue, while the other two bid her go hang herself, and are increasingly noisy and offensive, until at last their Ruler is exhausted, gives up, and surrenders."[6]

To better understand the powerful grasp that emotions have on the "reasoning brain," and why feelings and thoughts are so often in conflict, let's examine how the human brain (an organ that is triple in size to our nearest cousins in evolution—nonhuman primates) evolved.

The most primitive part of the human brain, shared with all species that have more than a minimal nervous system, is the brainstem surrounding the spinal cord. It can be thought of as a set of preprogrammed regulators that maintain basic functions of the body. From this most ancient root, and with the arrival of the first mammals, the "limbic system" emerged. It brought "emotions" to the brain's repertoire. Millions of years later in evolution, a new brain part developed.

86

Approximately 100 million years ago, mammalian brains had an immense growth spurt. Several new layers of brain cells were added to the ancient brain's thin two-layered cortex (the regions that plan, comprehend what is sensed, and coordinate movement) to form the neocortex. This new gray matter offered an extraordinary intellectual advantage.

The human neocortex, which is much larger than in any other species, is the seat of thought. It helps us put together and understand what the senses perceive. It enables us to think about our feelings and have feelings about ideas and symbolic depictions, like works of art and literature.

The neocortex can influence and moderate limbic system impulses. For example, a person may feel quite angry and want to physically strike someone for doing something that he or she perceives as a great affront. But rational thought (generated in the neocortex) can intervene and keep the aggrieved party from acting in ways that might be deleterious—for example, hitting or shooting the putative offender.

In some circumstances, rational thought may not be readily available to a person. For example:

- One may not have been taught how to think rationally under pressure.
- One may have learned irrational ways to handle different situations.
- One may be a victim of an "emotional hijacking," a situation in which the amygdala (a limbic system component, perched above the brainstem, that is involved in emotional processing) reroutes the neural transmissions that typically go from the thalamus to the neocortex to itself. This detour takes away the

ability of the neocortex to apply reason to sensory information.

Fortunately, with proper training, individuals can learn to overcome the aforementioned scenarios and think and behave in an emotionally intelligent manner.

"Thoughts" and "Feelings"

We live in a process world. But our language does not accurately reflect this fact because it allows us to "split" with words what cannot be split in the world "out there." For example, we talk about the mind and body as if they were separate entities. But that's not true. Can there be a mind without a body? Lacking a body, there would be no mind. And without the mind, what would the body be? Moreover, the chemical processes of the body affect the mind—that's why antidepressants work. And the opposite is true. Our mental state can influence our physical condition—worry can aggravate ulcers and other bodily ailments.

General semantics labels our tendency to use words in isolation as *elementalism*. We practice elementalism when we talk about feelings and thoughts as if they were distinct elements that can exist without each other. But the fact is they *do* influence each other. To underscore that idea, GS suggests putting quotation marks around the terms "feelings" and "thoughts."

Placing quotes around the term "emotional response" is also useful, as such a response is an end product of complex psycho-neuro-physiological reactions to internal and external stimuli. In general semantics parlance, a complex reaction like this would be labeled an *evaluational reaction*.

General semantics contains many ideas and formulations that can be used to rectify dysfunctional evaluational reactions and improve functional ones. Some will now be discussed and applied to the five domains of emotional intelligence.

Using GS to Enhance Emotional Intelligence

Goleman defines EI as encompassing the following five domains:[7]

1. Knowing one's emotions
2. Managing emotions
3. Motivating oneself
4. Recognizing emotions in others (empathy)
5. Handling relationships.

Individuals differ in their EI domain abilities. Some may be more proficient at interpersonal relating, while others may have greater self-awareness. But since the brain is quite plastic, and constantly learning, lapses in emotional skills can be remedied (to a great extent each EI domain represents a body of habit and response that, with the right effort, can be improved on).[8] The following descriptions show how general semantics tools and formulations can assist in that task.

Knowing One's Emotions

People who are in touch with their feelings can better understand their impulses to practice certain behaviors. Such knowledge is important, particularly if the impelling forces are negative ones (e.g., anxiety, excessive anger, timidity, etc.).

To be more mindful of one's emotions, general semantics advocates engaging in contemplation, *semantic relaxation* (a process for decreasing muscular tension), and sensory awareness.[9]

Such nonverbal methods can aid an individual to concentrate his or her whole being on identifying and understanding his or her feelings as they occur.

Using an *extensional orientation* (focusing on "the facts" rather than on assumptions) is another way to stay attentive to one's emotions, as it encourages analyzing phenomena rather than denying or disputing their existence. The scientific method is a particularly effective extensional approach. Since the time of Galileo, its methodology—observe, experiment, and evaluate—has brought about numerous advances in many different areas of human endeavor.

Albert Ellis, the founder of Rational Emotive Behavior Therapy, used the scientific method to overcome his fear of rejection when he was a college undergraduate. One weekend, he asked over one hundred women he did not know to go out with him. All but one turned him down, and she never showed up for the date, but he saw that he could live with rejection and this gave him confidence to persevere in trying to make contact with the opposite sex. Although practice didn't make perfect, Ellis claims he did have greater amatory success over time.

Managing One's Emotions

Those who learn to manage their emotions tend to tolerate frustration and stress better than those who are ineffective in this area. This gives them an advantage in completing long-term projects and getting along with others.

The *delayed-reaction technique*, a GS tool that involves delaying one's reactions to investigate matters before taking action, can be quite beneficial for emotional self-management. It allows time for rational thought to moderate potentially adverse *signal reactions* (a GS term for quick and unthinking responses). *Multi-*

valued reasoning, which will be discussed next, is another helpful GS emotional-self-management tool.

There is a longstanding tradition in studying emotions to describe them as positive or negative. This is sometimes reduced to the idea of pleasures and pain—or pleasure and no pleasure. But this either-or way of thinking about emotions misses the complexity that is involved with each emotion. *Multi-valued reasoning*, an attitude of "both-and" rather than "either-or," can capture such complexity.

For example, love is often considered the most positive emotion. But love also frequently leads to pain, jealousy, and anger. Anger is often at the top of the negative emotions, but Aristotle, who wrote at some length about anger, argues that anger is sometimes exactly the right response. (The assumption here is that anger is the right response to the right occasion to the right degree and directed at the right person. In such cases, Aristotle maintains, one would be a fool not to get angry.) And fear, which many people consider a negative emotion, may be our most valuable emotion. Without it we would perish. We can also enjoy fear, such as when we watch a horror movie.

Understanding that emotions are complex can help a person to better manage their feelings, as they will not be lead astray by simplistic assumptions regarding the "goodness" or "badness" of a particular emotion. The idea that emotions are complex, as has been shown, can come from a multi-valued reasoning process.

Motivating Oneself

Individuals who can marshal their emotions in the service of a goal have increased opportunities for achievement and life successes. Alfred Korzybski's *"happiness formula"* (realistic goals + hard work = happiness) provides a simple but effective prescription to realize such desired outcomes. Its application can also help one cultivate useful emotional habits, like being patient when things don't promptly pan out the way you want them to, and avoiding the *IFD disease*.

The IFD disease is a GS notion that describes a condition in which a person moves from a state of Idealization to Frustration to Demoralization. At the demoralization stage, it can be difficult to motivate oneself. To prevent IFD disease, GS recommends connecting language with real and specific possibilities. For example, rather than seeking a glorified ideal like "true happiness," which is a vague standard that has no objective referents in the "real world," one can consider "happiness" as a warm bagel with cream cheese or having your car start in the morning when the temperature is ten degrees. Or if it is not these things, happiness is something that you *do* or you can imagine yourself doing, something unambiguous and achievable.

Empathizing with Others

In his book, *The Explosive Child*, Dr. Ross Greene calls empathy the access code to a person's brain. Those who possess this code have a tremendous edge in interpersonal communications—people who feel understood are likely to reveal more of their deepest thoughts and feelings.

Since everyone's nervous system is unique, it can take real effort and concentration to accurately figure out what another person is feeling. GS suggests paying particular attention to nonverbal cues (e.g., tone of voice, posture, facial expression, etc.). Research indicates more than 80 percent of interpersonal communication is nonverbal.

Utilizing the GS notion that humans behave as *organisms-as-wholes-in-environments* (i.e., people react in complex ways in various circumstances) can also help us to sharpen our empathy skills by reminding us that since human reactions are complex, finding "emotional common ground" between individuals may be a formidable task. And accepting the idea that human responses are multifaceted can motivate us to be indefatigable and persevering with others if emotional common ground is not immediately discovered.

Handling Relationships

Individuals who are skilled in handling relationships can resolve conflicts and negotiate disagreements more effectively than those lacking this ability. To become more competent in dealing with people one can use *dating*, a GS technique that involves attaching dates to our evaluations of individuals and situations to remind us that human beings and relationships change over time. For example, Mary (this year) is not Mary (last year); my marriage (currently) is not my marriage (twenty years ago); my friend Mark (today) is not my friend Mark (tomorrow). Because people and relationships change it is important to modify our thinking and behavior to conform to present conditions, rather than using a cookie-cutter approach to interpersonal relations.

Another way to become more adept in dealing with people is to heed the advice of the eminent general semanticist Irving J. Lee, who asserted that we tend to discriminate against people to the degree that we fail to distinguish among them. *Indexing*, a GS tool that involves using mathematical subscripts to break down larger categories into their component parts, is a useful technique for addressing Lee's concern.

Finally, to show respect for another's feelings, general semantics suggests adopting a *"to me" attitude*—employing terms like "I think," "it seems," and "to me" when making statements. Such expressions make it clear that our observations and opinions have definite limits: For example, "I think New York is the best place to live." "It seems that it is going to rain today." "To me, macaroni and cheese is the most delicious food." The "to me" approach signals to others that we are not speaking with omniscient authority, but rather, with a tip of the hat to Buckminster Fuller, as fellow travelers on spaceship Earth.

Conclusion

Since its inception, general semantics has been quite involved with "emotional intelligence." *Science and Sanity* (1933), the book that launched GS, focused heavily on how to increase human cooperation and reduce human misery and Wendell Johnson's GS classic *People in Quandaries* (1946) had as its subtitle "The Semantics of Personal Adjustment." S. I. Hayakawa named his book *Language in Action* (1941) and Irving J. Lee wrote texts titled *Language Habits in Human Affairs* (1941) and *The Language of Wisdom and Folly* (1949). In the 1950s, J. Samuel Bois's concern with emotion was evident in the title he chose for his book *Explorations in Awareness* (1957). Today, the tradition continues, with GS volumes such as *Developing Sanity in Human Affairs* (1998), *Drive Yourself Sane* (2001), *Sensible Thinking for Turbulent Times* (2006), and *Practical Fairy Tales for Everyday Living* (2007), and with IGS web material that deals with educating people on the complex nature and inter-relatedness of thoughts and feelings.

PART 3

Going Beyond Similarities to Discover Differences that Make a Difference

General Semantics and Journalism Ethics

" An orientation to general semantics will raise the linguistic consciousness of journalists, bring them to a higher level of sophistication, instill in them a recognition of the weaknesses and the power of words, and generally help them overcome the enslaving tendencies of language."[1] So says John C. Merrill in *Journalism Ethics: Philosophical Foundations for News Media*, his comprehensive and well-researched book on morals in journalism.

In a chapter titled "Korzybski to the Rescue," Merrill notes that studying general semantics should have particular relevance for journalists, as words are the fundamental tools of their craft. He also presents specific GS ideas and observations pertinent for members of the fourth estate. The following are some of those ideas and observations plus additional material pertaining to general semantics and journalism ethics.

Some Basic GS Ideas Relevant to Journalism Ethics

The Word Is Not the Thing

General semanticists say, "The map is not the territory." The symbol is not the object or event that is symbolized. For example, when we describe a "flower" we should be aware the "real" flower is an ever-changing process that entails air, light, water, and soil. When using words, we should not fool ourselves into thinking we are fully describing an actual flower. The word is not the thing.

This principle is even more important when we are discussing abstract terms, as their lack of concrete referents can confuse and deceive. Such obfuscation and trickery is shown in the following exercise.

Instant Eloquence
Insert the words below, in any position, in the blanks.
peace, justice, freedom, truth, honor, wisdom

What we need today is not false _____ but old-fashioned _____. For surely, there is no real _____ without _____. And as our forefathers knew so well, the price of _____ is a little _____.

Stay Low on the Abstraction Ladder

In communicating with others, don't use abstract terms when you can use more meaningful—more specific—ones. For example, when expressions like *pornography, good Christians, arrogant government officials, fundamentalists,* or *concerned voters* are used in a story, it is helpful for the journalist to explain them. If possible, the journalist should give specific examples of what the subjects do or what they believe, in order to clarify a story's meaning.

Make Clear Distinctions: Reports, Inferences, and Judgments

Reports are based on observable data and are verifiable. A *report*: Bill Smith, age twenty-five, was sentenced last week to fifteen years in prison.

Inferences are assumptions made from known data. An *inference*: Bill Smith will soon be in prison.

Judgments are conclusions made from inferences. A *judgment*: Bill Smith is an evil and dangerous individual.

Journalists frequently confuse or mix reports, inferences, and judgments, which is unfortunate, as flawed inferences or flawed judgments can have a negative impact on "objective reporting."

Recognition of Non-Allness

One can never completely describe anything. Certain characteristics are always left out. For example, a report may say, "He is a New York attorney." But he is a great deal more (a husband, a Baptist, an alcoholic, an ex-military man, etc.). Journalists, when using language, must leave out much significant information. The issue for ethical reporters (ethical in the sense of a dedication to "truthful, accurate, and objective reporting") is that they should not intentionally bias their story by what is omitted, and they should be aware of the omissions.

Delay Your Reaction

A hunter lived with an infant in a cabin, guarded by his dog. One day the hunter returned from the fields and saw the cradle overturned and the baby nowhere in sight. The room was a mess. The dog had blood all over his muzzle. The hunter, enraged, shot the dog. He then found the baby unharmed under the bed and a dead wolf in the corner.

Uncritical assumptions can result in negative consequences. Ethical journalists understand this idea and so, following the general semantics recommendation to delay one's reaction to more accurately assess what is going on in situations, they do not precipitously rush when gathering facts for a story. Unlike many of us, such reporters do not take for granted the human ability to delay one's reaction. They know the capacity to delay reacting, and bring our higher brain functions into play, is a key characteristic that distinguishes our species from the rest of the animal kingdom.

Reality Is Dynamic

The Greek philosopher Heraclitus famously said one can not step in the same river twice. What he meant by this is life is perpetually in flux, people and situations are constantly shifting. While language may impose, as Nietzsche suggested, a "stabilizing fiction" on events that transpire in our restless universe, the fact is change is ever present. Because reality is dynamic, ethical reporters will not use an old quotation as if it were currently valid to give someone's views on a subject nor will they automatically assume the views individuals hold today are the same they espoused thirty years ago.

Person₁ Is Not Person₂

The eminent general semanticist Irving J. Lee said that we tend to discriminate against people to the degree that we fail to distinguish among them. *Indexing*, a GS tool that involves using mathematical subscripts to break down larger categories into their component parts, is an effective technique for addressing Lee's concern (e.g., $person_1$ is not $person_2$, is not $person_3$, is not $person_4$). Its use can remind journalists that members of the same group are not the same and that it is dangerous to make assumptions about individuals because of their nationality, race, religion, party, or other characteristics.

Multivalued Orientation

Aristotle's law of the excluded middle (A thing is either "A" or "not A") encourages us to think every question can be answered in terms of "either-or." The structure of the English language also pushes us in that direction. With its many polarizing terms (good/bad, tall/short, liberal/conservative, etc.), English supports reasoning through extremes rather than by gradations.

General semantics notes that either-or thinking keeps us from seeing the great diversity in the world. For example, as opposed to being tall or short, or liberal or conservative, most people fall "heightwise" and politically somewhere along a continuum. Ethical reporters are mindful that accurate descriptions of people and events involve more than just assigning them to one of two dichotomous categories.

Beware the "Is" of Projection

"She's a knockout." "That painting is not art." "*King Kong* was a great movie." When individuals make statements like these, they are telling us precious little about what they are describing. They are saying, instead, something about themselves. They are projecting their ideas of what they consider to be "beautiful," "art," and "outstanding cinema." They are confusing opinions with facts.

To demonstrate awareness that our thoughts or comments are products of our internal condition, rather than reports of external "reality," general semantics advocates the use of qualifying expressions like "it seems to me," "as I see it," "apparently," "from my point of view," etc. These phrases signal to others that we are transmitting personal observations about reality, not divine truths.

The "Meaning" of Words

What's the difference between a "freedom fighter" and a "terrorist?" Were the victims at the Abu Ghraib prison in Iraq subjected to "abuse" or "torture?" Are organizations that comment on news reporting "media watchdog groups," or are they "pressure groups?" Don't look to the dictionary to answer these questions. Their answers depend on how people perceive things.

General semantics observes that, strictly speaking, words don't "mean;" people do. The physicist P. W. Bridgman put it this way, "Never ask 'What does word X mean?' but ask instead, 'What do I mean when I say word X?' or 'What do you mean when you say word X?'"[2] Words do not have "one true meaning." For the five hundred most used words in the English language, the *Oxford Dictionary* lists 14,070 meanings.[3] Ethical journalists understand that conveying meaning is a complex and tricky matter and that possibilities for confusion are a constant threat.

Natural Penchant for Partiality

General semantics recognizes there is a tendency for individuals to select (or abstract) from reality those portions that are consistent with personal values. In reporting a story, a newsperson may choose what is appealing, what coincides with preferences, what gives pleasure. Ethical journalists guard against such egotistical inclinations and are able to force themselves to include information in stories that is uncongenial to them and with which they disagree.

GS Observations on Media Bias, Abstracting, Presentation, and Perception

Media Bias

In his book *Language in Thought and Action*, the general semanticist S. I. Hayakawa points out that when a newspaper carries a story we don't like, omitting facts we think are important and emphasizing certain facts we consider unfair, we are tempted to berate the paper for slanting the story.[4] But, he argues, we assume what seems important or unimportant to us would seem equally important or unimportant to the journalists. We are making an inference about the writer of the story or about the editors. The assumption of bias leads us to believe the editors purposely made the story misleading. Such an inference, according to Hayakawa, is not rational. It may well be our (the readers') bias is the problem in that the process of selection and abstraction imposed on us by our own interests and background is already slanted.

Yet there are cases when journalists deliberately slant stories. When they do this they are not giving us "good" maps of the territory—too much will be left out, and the map will tend to be one-dimensional and misleading. Ethical journalists will look at the same subject from many perspectives and will, therefore, be in a better position to draw for the reader a good map, one that is reliable.

Abstracting

Stuart Chase, the author of the *The Tyranny of Words* (an early and influential popularization of general semantics), suggests that in analyzing verbal passages we try to identify abstract words and phrases that don't have discoverable referents—and substitute a *blab* for every meaningless term.[5] He calls the *blab* a "semantics blank" where nothing of significance comes through. Journalists who use a high degree of "blab" language communicate very little.

One may take any newspaper or periodical and scrutinize a story for blab lingo. Merrill offers this hypothetical sentence for such analysis. "The American society today, steeped as it is in multicultural sham, has retreated into a dark abyss where every kind of verbal description is tinged with implied prejudice and other demeaning implications."[6] Translated into blab, this sentence would read, "The blab blab today, blabbed as it is in blab blab, has retreated into a blab blab, where every kind of blab blab is tinged with blab blab and blab blab." Blabbing compromises truthful, accurate, and objective reporting.

Presentation

Gregg Hoffmann, an award-winning journalist and the author of *Mapping the Media*—a media literacy guidebook based on general semantics formulations, notes that a news story goes through a process made necessary by the organization of media businesses. "Reporters collect information by observations in the field, or from secondary sources. They must then write or produce their story to a deadline, and fit it into a designated space in a newspaper, or a time limit for a newscast. Editors may cut the length or time of the story. They will write a headline and may add photos or charts for a newspaper. They may include graphics and video for TV."[7] Ethical reporters and editors remain vigilant to not let the process of the news business interfere with the objective of presenting fair and balanced news stories.

Perception

General semantics recognizes human perception is not a simple matter of stimulus-response (the human nervous system is the essential intermediary) nor is it ever complete. In their article "Using General Semantics Principles in the Basic News Reporting Classroom," Russell and Many offer this example: An "event" happens that occurs in the world. Reporter #1 comes to it and perceives it, or parts of it, and his or her perception of the event is different than that of reporter #2. What this signifies is there will always be differences in reports of the "same" news events.[8] But, say Russell and Many, "If they [journalism students and reporters] can be taught their observations are by definition incomplete, perhaps they will learn to ask even more questions and search for more sources and vantage points before concluding they have observed and reported everything."[9]

Conclusion

Merrill maintains that an orientation to general semantics will raise the linguistic consciousness of journalists, bring them to a higher level of sophistication, instill in them a recognition of the weaknesses and the power of words, and generally help them overcome the enslaving tendencies of language. He specifically says, with respect to the benefits of GS training for journalists: "most people hardly ever think about a Korzybskian emphasis. Therefore, they fall into poor language habits, that provide only a one-dimensional, inflexible world in which concepts are drawn in either-or terms and people and institutions are depicted as static, stereotyped entities. Most journalistic maps are poorly drawn; the lines are fuzzy and significant developments are left out. A new sensitivity to language coupled with a recognition of its potent impact on thinking and action, will enable journalists to be more ethical, to become more symbolically sophisticated, and to draw more progressively reliable maps of the complex and rugged territory of reality."[10]

9

Checking Conventional Maps of American History

There is an analogy in general semantics that words and statements are like maps that describe territories. The purpose of the analogy is to remind us that words, like maps, only *represent* reality and are not reality itself (the map is not the territory). To find out how well words represent reality, general semantics suggests it is a good idea to check the map against the territory—carefully examine what is being labeled or described to see if the words that describe it are accurate. Let's do that with respect to ten conventional verbal maps of American history.

Linguistic Maps and Territories

Christopher Columbus Discovered America

A review of the territory: A national American holiday and two centuries of school history lessons have led many to believe as true that Christopher Columbus was the first to reach America. But most scholars think Columbus actually landed in Cuba, Hispaniola (Haiti and the Dominican Republic), and on an island in the Bahamas during his 1492 voyage from Spain to the New World. Archaeological evidence suggests Norse sailors led by Leif Ericson reached North America five hundred years before Columbus, establishing a colony in Newfoundland around 1000 CE.

It is interesting to note that Columbus's bravery, persistence, and seamanship have earned him a prominent place in American history. But many schoolbooks gloss over the fact that in his obsessive quest for gold, he enslaved the local population. With other Spanish adventurers, as well as later European colonizers, Columbus opened an era of genocide that decimated the Native American population through warfare, forced labor, and European diseases to which the Indians, a name Columbus bestowed on Native Americans, had no natural immunities.

Considering Columbus's prominence in our nation's history, one might ask, why don't we live in the United States of Columbus? The answer is that Amerigo Vespucci, an Italian who captained four voyages to the "New World" beginning in 1499, recognized that the New World, a term he coined, was a landmass separate from Asia. To honor his revelation, Vespucci's given name was placed on the first map of the region. While Columbus may have found the new world first, Vespucci understood it was a new world. Columbus went to his grave thinking he had reached Asia.

The Pilgrims Landed on Plymouth Rock

A review of the territory: On December 16, 1620, the Pilgrims on the *Mayflower* reached their new home in America. Nearly all scholars put the Pilgrims' landing about ten miles north of the lumpy scrap of stone known as Plymouth Rock. There is no mention in any historical account of that rock—a large boulder located in Plymouth, Massachusetts, into which, in 1880, the Pilgrim Society carved the year 1620.

The legend of Plymouth Rock was started in 1741 by a ninety-five-year-old man who said his father told him about it. Twenty-eight years later, celebrating the Pilgrims' landing at Plymouth Rock became an annual event in New England. By

1835, Alexis de Tocqueville reported pieces of the rock were being venerated in different American cities, and it was established as an American icon.

Offers for chunks of Plymouth Rock have occasionally popped up on eBay where asking prices have been as much as $900. However, while it is true lots of souvenir hunters did carve off parts of the Rock during the eighteenth and nineteenth centuries, there is no way to differentiate a real hunk of Plymouth Rock from a fake one. For those interested in seeing what's left of Plymouth Rock, which is only about one-third to one-half of its original size, it is preserved today in a state park near the mouth of Plymouth Harbor.

Betsy Ross Sewed the First American Flag

A review of the territory: The legend of Betsy Ross as the first embroiderer of the American flag was originally brought to light in 1870 when one of her grandsons, William J. Canby, reported a story his grandmother had told him. According to Canby, George Washington and several others visited Betsy's upholstery shop in Philadelphia and showed her a crude drawing of the flag, which she then produced. After Canby's death, a book called *The Evolution of the American Flag,* published in 1909, presented the claims for Betsy Ross made by Canby in 1870.

While Betsy Ross did make some flags in the late eighteenth century, it is known she made "ship's colors" for which she was paid, no one has been able to verify that the Canby story is true. Furthermore, some evidence exists that a Philadelphia poet named Francis Hopkinson designed the Stars and Stripes in 1780. However, Betsy Ross is still thought of by most as the sewer of the first American flag, and her house in Philadelphia has become a historical site. Interestingly, there is doubt among some historians that she ever lived in that house.

Paul Revere Single-handedly Stirred a Sleeping Countryside to Arms

A review of the territory: "Listen my children and you shall hear / Of the midnight ride of Paul Revere." These words, penned by Henry Wadsworth Longfellow in a poem published in 1861, boosted the legend of a lone rider who helped start the Revolutionary War. The problem is, the poem is highly inaccurate.

Firstly, Revere was not alone in warning the local militias. Another man, William Dawes, a Boston tanner, took the main road out of town. Revere, meanwhile, managed with the help of several other people to sneak across the Charles River.

In Longfellow's poem, Revere is portrayed as waiting for a signal from the Old North Church ("Two if by sea"). But in descriptions of his ride that he wrote after the battles, Revere said he had arranged for the lanterns to be lit while he was still in Boston—two of them, to indicate the British would be traveling by sea—in case he wasn't able to cross the river. The citizens of Charlestown, on the other side, dispatched their own rider to spread the news. Historians aren't sure what became of the third rider.

Later that night, Longfellow's poem depicts Revere galloping into Concord to sound the alarm. But Revere said he never made it that far. He left Lexington with Dawes and they met another rider, Samuel Prescott, along the way. Before they reached town, British officers stopped the three men. Dawes and Prescott got away, but Revere was captured. Prescott was the only one who got to Concord. Revere, in fact, was neither alone nor the man who completed his mission.

The Civil War Was a Clash between Two Diametrically Opposed Groups

A review of the territory: After the first seven states seceded there were eight slave states left, and the US government tried to craft a compromise to keep the Union intact. While the lower South states where slavery was more deeply entrenched were solidly secessionist, voters in Virginia, Arkansas, and Missouri elected a majority of pro-Unionists to state conventions to decide the question. In North Carolina and Tennessee, the voters rejected secession conventions entirely. And in Texas, Governor Sam Houston, the greatest hero of Texas independence, opposed secession. Clearly, not everyone in the south wanted to leave the Union.

In the North, a number of people, including the prominent abolitionist Horace Greeley and lots of workingmen who believed freeing the slaves would mean lower wages, argued that the North should allow the South to go its own way. Other Northerners wanted to preserve the Union for economic reasons. For example, many Northern businessmen believed losing the South would mean economic catastrophe. In fact, the question of secession in the North and the South involved a multiplicity of views.

Abraham Lincoln Said, "You Can Fool All the People Some of the Time..."

A review of the territory: One of the most famous quotes attributable to Lincoln is this one: "If you once forfeit the confidence of your fellow citizens, you can never regain their respect. You can fool all the people some of the time and some of the people all of the time, but you cannot fool all of the people all of the time." But there is no record Lincoln ever really said it. Supposedly part of a September 1858 speech in Clinton, Illinois, the quotation does not show up in the text printed in the local newspaper. The best evidence available for attributing the quote to Lincoln came from two people who in 1910 recollected what Lincoln had said in his Clinton speech.

The Illinois Historic Preservation Agency has a page on its Web site that exposes sayings Lincoln never made. Among them:

- "To sin by silence, when they should protest, makes cowards of men."
- "There is no honorable way to kill, no gentle way to destroy. There's nothing good in war except its ending."
- "The strength of a nation lies in the homes of its people."

Lincoln also never said "If I knew what brand he'd used, I'd send every general a bottle," in response to General Ulysses S. Grant's drinking.

Teddy Roosevelt Led the Rough Riders Cavalry Charge that Won the Battle of San Juan Hill

A review of the territory: The Rough Riders were a cavalry regiment Teddy Roosevelt recruited to take part in the Spanish-American War. It was a widely varied force consisting of seasoned ranch hands, Pawnee scouts, Ivy League athletes, cowboys, policemen, east-coast polo players, and others who represented a broad cross-section of American society.

Before leaving for Cuba, rigorous cavalry training was conducted for about a month at Camp Wood in San Antonio, Texas. The Rough Riders then moved to Tampa, Florida, the port of embarkation for the Cuban Campaign. Unfortunately, a serious lack of transport resulted in almost all of the unit's horses being left behind.

The regiment landed near Daiquiri, Cuba, on June 22, 1898 as part of the Fifth Corps Cavalry Division under the command of Major General Joseph Wheeler. Although officially a cavalry unit, the regiment fought on foot.

The Rough Riders were only a few hundred men out of eight thousand US soldiers who took part in the battle of San Juan Hill. Actually, about 1,200 African-Americans, known then as "Buffalo Soldiers," had as much to do with the victory as the Rough Riders. But Roosevelt's account of the battle emphasized and expanded the role the Rough Riders played, and his chronicle of events helped him to get elected president in 1903.

American Women Were not Allowed to Vote before the Passage of the Nineteenth Amendment in 1920

A review of the territory: The Nineteenth Amendment was not as revolutionary as it may seem. Women in New Jersey had been granted the right to vote as early as 1776. At that time, a new state constitution was adopted that gave the suffrage to any free person worth more than fifty pounds. If a woman met that financial qualification, she could vote. (The men who framed the New Jersey constitution had not expected women to take advantage of the vote and were not trying to make the state more democratic. But their constitution inadvertently did open up the system to women—at least women who had more than fifty pounds.)

At first, few women availed themselves of the opportunity to cast a ballot. Legislators believed the constitutional loophole so harmless it was retained when a new constitution was written in 1797. But the next few years saw women deciding closely contested elections and so, in 1807, the New Jersey legislature rescinded women suffrage.

In 1868, the issue of women suffrage reemerged in the

Wyoming Territory. Without controversy, a measure granting women full rights passed the upper house of the legislature. However in the lower house the bill faced stern opposition. Men there ridiculed the bill, added outrageous amendments, and considered not voting on it until July 4, 1870—when the legislature would no longer be in session. But the bill passed by a majority of six to four. (The members voting for the measure did not really want women voting but since they were all Democrats they decided it would be politically advantageous to let the governor, a Republican, who was known to oppose woman suffrage, veto the bill. He then, and not they, would be blamed for defeating women's rights.)

But Republican governor John Campbell did not take the bait. Though a young man and new to the state, he detected the plot, and not willing to incur the wrath of the ladies, on December 10, 1869, he signed the suffrage bill. At the time of the passage of the Nineteenth Amendment, women were allowed to vote in a dozen states.

John F. Kennedy Wrote *Profiles in Courage*, for which He Was Awarded a Pulitzer Prize in 1957

A review of the territory: It is true Kennedy won a Pulitzer Prize for *Profiles in Courage*, a book about senators who had performed a courageous act while in office. It is also true the book won Kennedy national attention and cemented his standing among liberals in the Democratic Party. But it is highly questionable whether he wrote it, or at least wrote it by himself.

The idea for the book—a study of heroic US senators—came to Kennedy in 1954, when he was a first-term senator. Initially, he imagined it as a magazine article, but during a long convalescence after a couple of back operations he decided to make it into a book. His chief assistant on the project was his speechwriter Ted Sorensen, who worked on the project for six months, sometimes twelve hours a day. Sorensen coordinated the work and drafted many chapters. Others also made contributions, most importantly Georgetown history professor Jules Davids.

Some historians have argued that JFK was the author of the book in the sense that he "authorized" it. While it is true Kennedy conceived the book and supervised its production, he did little of the research and writing. Evidence also exists that suggests *Why England Slept*, an earlier bestselling book on the causes of World War II credited to Kennedy, was at least partly the work of someone else.

The Bush Administration Moved the United States away from a Tradition of Cooperative Diplomacy through Foreign-government Overthrows

A review of the territory: America has had a long history of toppling foreign regimes. Beginning with the ouster of Hawaii's monarchy in 1893 and continuing through the Spanish-American War, the Cold War, and the "war on terror," the United States (through coups, revolutions, and invasions) has overthrown fourteen foreign governments. Specifically, those in Hawaii, Cuba, the Philippines, Puerto Rico, Nicaragua, Honduras, Iran, Guatemala, South Vietnam, Chile, Grenada, Panama, Afghanistan, and Iraq.

In the late nineteenth and early twentieth century, the United States carried out overthrow operations openly, through military power. During the Cold War, that was no longer possible because an invasion or direct intervention against a foreign government might bring about a reaction from the Soviet Union. Therefore in the early 1950s, the CIA was given the job of clandestinely overthrowing governments. It did so four times in Iran, Guatemala, South Vietnam, and Chile.

In recent decades, America has returned to its original way of overthrowing foreign governments: by military invasion. During this period, the United States has overthrown the administrations of Grenada, Panama, Afghanistan, and Iraq.

America will probably remain an interventionist power. Its position in the world makes this fairly certain. But an important question to ask is: Can the United States intervene more effectively, in ways that promote stability rather than instability? Perhaps if our leaders are able to learn from their mistakes in the past, the answer to that question will be yes.

10

A General Semantics Analysis of the *RMS Titanic* Disaster

And as the smart ship grew
In stature, grace, and hue,
In shadowy silent distance
grew the Iceberg too.
— Thomas Hardy, *The Convergence of the Twain*

*R*MS *Titanic*, the largest moving object of its time, began its maiden voyage from Southampton, England to New York City on Wednesday, April 10, 1912. On Sunday, April 14th, the temperature of the Atlantic Ocean fell to near freezing; the night was clear and calm. The ship's captain had received various ice warnings from other vessels, some of which reached him while others did not.

At 11:40 p.m., while sailing about 400 miles south of the Grand Banks of Newfoundland, lookouts spotted a large iceberg directly in the *Titanic's* path. The ship turned left to avoid the berg, but the massive chunk of ice opened mortal holes on the vessel's starboard side. The captain ordered lifeboats deployed and distress signals sent out.

Many of the lifeboats were launched at less than full capacity and a woman-and-children-first policy was the rule for coming aboard. At 2:20 a.m. the *Titanic* sank beneath the waves, a sinking that ended in the deaths of over 1,500 people and the start of a public fascination with a disaster filled with hubris, heartbreak and heroism. This chapter examines many significant aspects of that disaster through the formulations of general semantics.

A GS Analysis of the *RMS Titanic* Disaster

The Map Is Not the Territory
An Unsinkable Ship—Not Really

In 1912, the year it sank, the *Titanic* was known as the finest ship afloat. It weighed over 46,000 tons, was as high as an eleven-story building, and was 883 feet long from bow to stern (about a sixth of a mile). It had twenty-nine boilers, 159 furnaces, and a maximum speed of twenty-four knots. The *Titanic* was considered so well constructed that many nautical experts thought the ship virtually unsinkable.

The *Titanic* was reported to be watertight. It had a double bottom (the hull was built with two coats of steel) and was divided into sixteen watertight compartments separated by bulkheads pierced by a series of doors that were controlled either by automatic floating switches or by command from the bridge.

On the night of April 14th, when the *Titanic* hit the iceberg, water begun flooding into at least five of its "watertight compartments" that were anything but watertight as the bulkhead walls did not rise appreciably above the waterline. Water coming over the bulkhead walls could cascade into other compartments, which is what happened the night the *Titanic* went under. (The *Titanic* was designed to stay afloat with any two watertight compartments or its first four bow compartments flooded, but that number was exceeded in the collision. As its forward compartments filled, the *Titanic* began to go down at the head, and water rose and spilled into successive "watertight" compartments, much like water spilling into adjoining sections of a tilted ice-cube tray. Sinking became inevitable.)

Another factor that contributed to the *Titanic's* foundering was that the ship's builder had not used the highest quality wrought-iron rivets in welding the vessel's steel plates so when the *Titanic* hit the iceberg its rivet heads were more easily sheared off causing the plates that the rivets were holding to separate. Also, the expansion joints (mechanical assemblies that allow a ship's casing to flex in heavy seas) on the *Titanic* were poorly designed, which, even if the vessel had not struck an iceberg, made the ship vulnerable to stresses on its superstructure. Unsinkable the *Titanic* definitely was not, and sink it did.

Following the Titanic disaster, the company that operated the *Titanic*, the White Star Line, modified the design of the *Titanic's* sister ships in two ways: the double bottoms were extended up the sides of the hull and the transverse bulkheads of the watertight compartments were raised.

All the News Isn't Necessarily Fit to Print

Radio communication was in its formative years in 1912, and there was a great deal of confusion in England and the United States over the fate of the *Titanic*. Because of garbled messages, several newspapers published sketchy information as unvarnished truth by reporting that all the passengers had been saved and that the ship was being towed to Halifax, Nova Scotia. Both the *New York Evening Sun* and the *Boston Evening Transcript* made this error. William Randolph Hearst's *New York Journal*, which had the boldest headline of any newspaper, declared "ALL SAFE ON THE *TITANIC*."

But one paper put out information that was highly accurate from the start. *The New York Times* headline on April 15th, the day of the sinking, read "NEW LINER *TITANIC* HITS ICEBERG; SINKING BY THE BOW AT MIDNIGHT; WOMEN PUT OFF IN LIFEBOATS; LAST WIRELESS AT 12:27 A.M. BLURRED" and its entire front page was devoted to as many of the details as were known. The *Times* went on to earn national and international notice for its meticulous and comprehensive coverage of the "story of the century." The April 15th edition is considered by many media mavens to be the most important single issue leading to the creation of the *Times* as a global authority.

Seeing Should Not Always Be Believing
Although only three funnels were needed, a fourth "dummy" funnel was added to the *Titanic* by the White Star Line so the public would not perceive the four-funnel ships *Mauritania* and *Lusitania*, which were faster than the *Titanic* and the pride and joy of the Cunard Line, as being more powerful.

The Value of Delayed Reactions
Slapdash Supervision
Binoculars were issued to the lookouts on the *Titanic* on its trip from Belfast to Southampton. But during a last minute shakeup of personnel they were removed from the crow's nest and not replaced for the transatlantic voyage, thus the lookouts were unable to scour the sea for icebergs with field glasses during the crossing. When the ship's Second Officer, Charles Lightoller, was questioned at an inquiry about the lookouts not having binoculars he downplayed the matter saying that binoculars can be a liability in maintaining a sharp vigil. However, other experts, including the renowned Arctic explorer Admiral Robert Peary,

disagreed.

While it is impossible to go back and test the binoculars that were issued to the *Titanic*, to see how they would have performed in the low light conditions that were prevalent the night the ship took its last dive, they may have proven helpful to the lookouts in spotting dangers on the sea. That is what Frederick Fleet, the lookout who reported the iceberg to the *Titanic*'s bridge, said at a Senate hearing on the disaster. He maintained if he had been equipped with binoculars the night of the tragedy the collision could have been avoided, which leads one to wonder if the *Titanic* might have had a different fate if the officers responsible for supplying the lookouts with binoculars would have taken some extra moments to consider the merits of such devices and made sure the lookouts had them.

Reckless Speed

At the time of the calamity it is thought the *Titanic* was at its normal cruising speed of around 22 knots (approximately 25.3 mph), which was a bit under its top speed of about 24 knots (approximately 27.6 mph). However, not all ships were traveling at such a rapid pace in the area contiguous to the *Titanic* on its luckless night. The skipper of the *SS Californian*, which was anchored less than twenty miles from where the *Titanic* went down, had prudently decided to heave to.

But the captain of the *Titanic*, Edward J. Smith, elected to sprint toward his final port of call on the evening of April 14th, even though there was no moon, wind, or swell to help spot icebergs and the *Titanic* had received a number of wireless warnings earlier in the day from ships in front of it about bergs ahead—it seems Smith did not appreciate the value of wireless as a constant, continuous navigation aid. Captain Smith clearly wanted to reach New York City on schedule. (Some reasons for that: There was lots of competition for sea-going passengers in 1912 and punctual performance was a good selling point. J. Bruce Ismay, the head of the White Star Line, was aboard the *Titanic* and Smith's boss would have been happy about getting to New York on or ahead of time. This was Captain Smith's last trip before retiring and he may have wanted to finish his career with a flourish.)

If Captain Smith had delayed his reflexive desire to maintain normal cruising speed and instead had given added thought to the risks of moving quickly on iceberg-laden waters perhaps he might have concluded that slowing his ship down would be a wise thing to do. Such a conclusion could have resulted in a more beneficial outcome for the *Titanic*, as a slower speed would have given the ship's lookouts a better chance to see the iceberg and the ship a better chance of surviving the crash. With more thought Smith might have also decided to alter his course further to the south, post extra lookouts, and warn his engineers to be ready for emergency engine orders from the bridge. Regrettably, and to the great detriment of the crew and passengers aboard the *Titanic*, such actions were never taken.

The Importance of Accurate Assumptions
Foolhardy Pre-Sail Assumptions

The operators of the *Titanic* assumed that the technology and leadership on board the vessel was of such high quality that rigorous preparation for the ship's maiden voyage was unnecessary. Evidence of that lack of rigor includes the following: The sea trials of the *Titanic* took place just ten days before its initial trip, and lasted no more than twelve hours over the course of a day (the *Olympic*, a sister ship to the *Titanic*, received two days of sea trials). During these trials, the ship was never run at full speed (the *Olympic's* sea trials included several high-speed runs). A number of the crew did not join the ship until hours before its first, and last, commercial voyage. There were no lifeboat drills before the *Titanic* set sail for New York.

Had the White Star Line been less confident and more vigilant in their preparations for the *Titanic's* transatlantic journey it is likely more lives would have been saved after the ship struck the iceberg because its crew would have had added training in dealing with emergency situations. Moreover, if the *Titanic's* officers had been given further time to practice steering the ship during its sea trials the crash with the iceberg might have been avoided altogether, as they would have had a better chance to fathom that a huge vessel like the *Titanic* does not respond quickly to the helm. Possessed with that knowledge, the captain might have cut back speed when he was informed of bergs ahead on April 14th.

The *Titanic* may have also been able to miss the iceberg if First Officer William Murdoch, who was on bridge duty when the berg was sighted, had not requested the engines be reversed, prior to steering the ship to the left, as reversing the engines decreased the forward motion of the *Titanic* causing it to turn more slowly. Additionally, if Murdoch had opted to collide head on with the iceberg the *Titanic's* bow would have undoubtedly sustained major damage but the ship almost certainly would not have sunk—in 1907 the *Kronprinz Wilhelm,* a German liner, rammed an iceberg but was able to complete its voyage despite suffering a crushed bow.

Flawed Signal Readings
The night the *Titanic* sank, crewmembers on the *Californian* (a cargo steamer that Lord Mersey, the man in charge of the British Board of Trade Inquiry into the *Titanic* disaster, surmised was five to ten miles from the *Titanic*) observed lights from a "mystery ship." The sighting was made known to the

Californian's captain, Stanley Lord, who concurred that a Morse-lamp signal be send to that ship. The other vessel never replied.

A short while later, at 1:15 a.m., Captain Lord was stirred from slumber and informed that rockets were being fired from a ship in the vicinity of the *Californian*. Lord asked the crewman who had seen the rockets if they had been a company signal. The crewmember replied he didn't know. Lord said to keep signaling the ship by Morse lamp but did not request the vessel be contacted by wireless. He then went back to sleep.

Ships in the *Titanic* era sometimes fired flares and Roman candles at night for communication. By firing these in various colors each ship was identified. The night the *Titanic* went under it sent up eight white-exploding flares over the course of an hour at regular intervals. No company had as distress signals only white rockets or white rockets throwing off stars. Furthermore, rockets fired off one at a time at short intervals were internationally agreed to be distress signals.

Had Lord given the situation the benefit of a doubt he could have discovered if the mystery ship's rockets were distress signals by waking his radio operator and having him ascertain whether distress messages were coming in over the wireless. He then would have known of the *Titanic's* plight and could have steamed off to help rescue its passengers. Alas, Captain Lord chose not to rouse his radio operator, or himself, hence he did not learn of the tragedy until 6 a.m., when he heard from another ship about the sinking and when it was far too late to save anyone in the water. The *Carpathia*, which had rushed at top speed from fifty-eight miles away, was already picking up survivors.

After the *Titanic* disaster, it was agreed that rockets at sea would be interpreted as distress signals only, thus removing any possible misinterpretation from other vessels. Lamentably, that agreement came too late to help the poor souls on the *Titanic*.

"Women and Children First" Conjectures

Second Officer Charles Lightoller was in charge of loading the lifeboats on the port side of the *Titanic* and First Officer William Murdoch was in command on the starboard side. Both officers filled the boats using Captain Smith's policy directive of women and children first. However, each man interpreted the evacuation order differently; Murdoch took it to mean women and children *first* while Lightoller thought it meant women and children *only*. Consequently, Lightoller lowered lifeboats with empty seats if there were no women and children waiting to board, while Murdoch allowed a limited number of men to board if all the nearby women and children had embarked.

The women and children first rule, which was honored by most men on the ship and produced an overall death toll of nine men for every one woman, dealt a serious blow to the women's suffrage movement and the related cause of women's rights, both up-and-coming ideas in the first two decades of the twentieth century. The cry of "Votes for women!" seemed not so compelling when set against that of "Women and children first," a decree that was put into practice and went unchallenged by nearly all the women aboard the *Titanic* (some feminists were outraged that women may have let themselves be treated as helpless objects). Equality of rights also brought with it equality of risks; a notion that the suffragettes and women's rights advocates of the time, unlike women fifty years afterward, had not adequately considered.

The Assumptions of George Bernard Shaw and Sir Arthur Conan Doyle

George Bernard Shaw and Sir Arthur Conan Doyle published a series of letters in the *Daily News and Leader* in May 1912, expressing opposing views on the *Titanic* disaster. The first letter was written by Shaw, who railed against the British press for "outrageous romantic lying" on matters regarding the sinking. He specifically argued that the women and children first policy was not strictly followed; that Captain Smith, rather than being a superhero for going down with the ship, had been the precipitator of the accident by having his vessel speed through an ice field and having no binoculars for the lookouts; that lifeboats did not rescue people in the water because their occupants were afraid they would jeopardize their own lives by doing that; and that it was wrong to elevate preventable tragedies into badges of national honor. (Shaw particularly objected to the "canonizing" of Captain Smith for his supposed heroism and the myth that all the Englishmen aboard the ship had met death without a tremor.)

Doyle replied to Shaw by accusing him of deliberate misrepresentation and perversity. Yes, Captain Smith had made a mistake but he had given his life in recompense. The women and first policy was for the most part observed. The conduct of the American males aboard the ship was every bit as noble as that of their British counterparts. And courage and discipline should be honored when it is demonstrated in its highest form.

One can argue that Shaw and Doyle both made valid points. For example, it is true that lots of journalists outrageously romanticized the sinking. Nevertheless, many passengers and crew behaved with great dignity in the face of death. And while it would be wrong to say that only the Americans and British on board acted bravely throughout the disaster, we don't know much about how everyone else on the *Titanic* reacted because their stories were not reported on—of forty-three survivor accounts in the New York *Herald,* only two were steerage experiences. Suppositions about how the bulk of the *Titanic's* more than 2,000 passengers responded during the ship's last moments must be left to our individual imaginations, as must surmises about how we ourselves would have behaved during those terrible hours.

Indexing

Iceberg₁ Is Not Iceberg₂

Icebergs are commonly regarded as white. But not all icebergs are that color. When a melting iceberg becomes top heavy and rolls over it turns dark blue until the water runs out of it. At night, icebergs undergoing this change are quite hard to see. The iceberg that struck the *Titanic* was most likely one of these "blue" icebergs. It was invisible until it was just a third of a mile away and there were witnesses who testified at inquiries that were held following the disaster who said that it looked dark as it passed the ship.

Passenger₁ Is Not Passenger₂ Is Not Passenger₃

The *Titanic's* passengers were divided into three classes, determined not only by the price of their ticket, but by their wealth and social position. Individuals traveling in first class, the wealthiest passengers on board, included the cream of American and British society. Among the *Titanic's* first-class passengers were John Jacob Astor IV (who was worth well over $100 million in 1912, which would make him a multi-billionaire in today's world), George Widener (after the *Titanic* tragedy his wife donated a library at Harvard University in her son's name), Isidor Straus (co-owner of Macy's Department store), Benjamin Guggenheim (he became famous for spending his final hours changing into formal evening wear in order to die with dignity as a gentleman), and Mrs. Margaret Tobin Brown (a woman who posterity has dubbed "The Unsinkable Molly Brown"—the nickname refers to the help she rendered in the ship's evacuation and her insistence that Lifeboat No. 6 go back to look for survivors).

Second-class passengers were middle-class individuals and included teachers, writers, clergymen, and tourists. Third-class passengers, or "steerage" as the class was popularly labeled, were mainly immigrants moving to the United States and Canada.

First-class passengers resided on five levels from the upper to the promenade decks. They had easy or relatively easy access to the boat deck where all the lifeboats were housed. Sixty percent of first-class passengers survived the sinking, as did two "first-class pets," a Pomeranian and a Pekinese, who accompanied their owners into lifeboats.

Second-class passengers were located on the middle, upper, and saloon decks. Where second-class passengers were on the same deck as first-class passengers, the second-class passengers were further aft. More by social than physical barriers, many second-class passengers would have refrained from entering the first-class section of the boat deck. Forty-two percent of second-class passengers survived the sinking.

Third-class passengers had rooms on the lower decks of the ship and, with a few exceptions, had no direct or immediate access to lifeboats on the boat deck. Some gates separating the third-class section of the ship from the other areas, like the one leading from the aft well deck to the second-class section, were locked. Numerous third-class passengers who made it through the disaster did so only by reaching the last of the lifeboats that were launched. Twenty-five percent of third-class passengers survived the sinking.

Class distinctions were followed in death as in life. After the *Titanic* went down, the cable ship *Mackay-Bennett* gathered floating corpses in the water. The bodies of first-class passengers were put into coffins on deck, while those of the second and third class were sewn into canvas bags and stored on ice in the hold. Survivors on the rescue-ship *Carpathia* also observed class divisions by coming ashore from that steamer in class-order.

The Importance of Radio Operator$_n$

There were two wireless operators on the *Titanic*. Jack Phillips, age twenty-five, was the senior operator and Harold Bride, age twenty-two, was his assistant. The men, who made less than $300 each per year, worked in a small windowless room and had to keep the wireless operating round the clock. Between shifts they slept on bunks in a tiny space next door.

Phillips and Bride signed Ship's Articles and were therefore part of the crew and under the captain's command. But their chief devotion was to their employer, Marconi International Marine Communication Company Limited, an outfit that made most of its profits from sending Marconigram messages of the "Having a wonderful time, wish you were here" variety.

About 9 a.m. on Sunday April 14th, the *Titanic* received an ice advisory from the Cunard liner *Caronia* that told of field ice ahead. Around twenty minutes before noon the Dutch liner *Noordam* reported ice in much the same area and at 1:41 p.m. a warning of ice from the *SS Baltic* was received. A German ship, the *Amerika*, conveyed a message that it had passed two large bergs at 1:45 p.m. Not all these warnings were given to the officers navigating the *Titanic*.

The wireless stopped working around midday on Sunday, April 14th and Phillips and Bride spent the next seven hours locating the problem and making repairs. They got the wireless functioning again just a little after 7 p.m. and Phillips began to deal with the backlog of passenger messages that had collected at his desk.

Shortly after 9:30 p.m., Phillips received an ice warning from the *SS Mesaba* that a large number of icebergs, heavy pack ice, and an ice field lay in the path of the *Titanic*. Phillips, who was busily occupied transmitting passenger messages, did not send the warning to the bridge. Had Captain Smith known of that warning, which contained a detailed reading of the dangerous ice conditions in the area surrounding the *Titanic*, he might have considered changing course or reducing speed.

Around 11 p.m., less than an hour before the *Titanic* hit the iceberg that sank it, Phillips was once more interrupted by another ship, the *SS Californian*. The *Californian's* wireless operator relayed that his vessel was encircled by ice and had stopped. The *Californian* was quite close and the signal came in very loudly over Phillips' headphones, which led him to respond "Shut up!" and to put the message aside for later delivery. This communication was also not forwarded to the bridge, which was most unfortunate because if heeded it could have prevented the *Titanic's* sinking.

At 11:30 p.m., a half hour after he had imparted his ice update to the *Titanic*, the *Californian's* radio operator switched off his set and went to bed for the night. As a result he missed the wireless distress signals that were sent from the *Titanic* forty-five minutes later, an incredibly unlucky happening, as the *Californian* was close by and could have helped save people.

Following an investigation into the *Titanic* disaster, the US Congress passed the Radio Act of 1912. This law, along with the International Convention for the Safety of Life at Sea, mandated that radio communications on passenger ships be operated 24/7 along with a secondary power supply, so as not to miss distress calls. The Radio Act also compelled ships to maintain contact with vessels in their vicinity and coastal onshore radio stations. And it called for all US radio operators to be licensed by the

Martin H. Levinson

Department of Commerce and Labor. This latter proviso meant that to fulfill federal guidelines, radio operator$_1$, radio operator$_2$, radio operator$_3$, and all radio operators going forward had to operate in a standardized manner, as radio operator$_n$ so to speak. (NB: Pay for wireless operators also substantially increased and working conditions were improved.)

Dating
Steamships (1894) Are Not Steamships (1912)

No one thing relating to the huge loss of life from the *Titanic*'s sinking has provoked more fury than that the ship did not carry enough lifeboats for *all* its crew and passengers. The most recent law concerning lifeboats dated from 1894 and required a minimum of sixteen lifeboats for ships over 10,000 tons. This law had been established when the largest vessels afloat were the 12,950-ton-Cunarder *RMS Lucania* and her identically weighted sister *RMS Campania*. Since then, the size of ships had dramatically increased without a corresponding boost in lifeboat requirements, the consequence being that the 46,328-ton *Titanic* was legally required to carry only enough lifeboats for less than half its capacity.

The White Star Line actually exceeded regulations by including four collapsible lifeboats, providing a total capacity of 1,178 people, which amounted to about a third of *Titanic*'s total capacity of 3,547. As there were around 2,200 passengers on the *Titanic*'s maiden voyage even had its lifeboats been fully loaded, which they were not (only 705 people were loaded or made it on to the lifeboats the night of the tragedy), more than 1,000 passengers would not have been able to board them.

Some of the lifeboats were lowered half full, in large part because many of the passengers believed that the "unsinkable" *Titanic* was itself a lifeboat and the crew, which was new to the

129

ship and had not been told that the lifeboats could be safely loaded at full capacity, was afraid if the lifeboats were full that the added weight would cause them to buckle while they were suspended over the side.

For the first hour many passengers did not take the order to get into lifeboats all that seriously. They preferred the comfort and warmth of the ship to sitting in a small, exposed rowboat on the open seas. Also, there had been no lifeboat drills on the voyage so people did not know which boats they had been assigned to or how to get to those boats quickly in an emergency.

It had been presumed that if a serious accident occurred in the well-traveled North Atlantic sea-lanes, assistance from other vessels would be close by. Lifeboats then would be used to ferry passengers and crew from the incapacitated ship to its rescuers. Having enough lifeboats on the stricken vessel to accommodate all its passengers was considered superfluous to support this activity.

After the *Titanic* disaster, recommendations were made by both British and American authorities that (a) ships would carry enough lifeboats for those aboard, (b) mandated lifeboat drills would be implemented, and (c) lifeboat inspections would be conducted. These recommendations were incorporated into a global maritime safety treaty known as the International Convention for the Safety of Life at Sea, which took effect in 1914. (Nowadays, due partly to the *Titanic's* tragic loss of life, cruise ships must have enough lifeboats to hold 25 percent more people than the total number of passengers and crew on board.)

Alexander Carlisle, the chairman of the managing directors from Harland and Wolff, the firm that built the *Titanic,* had originally planned for sixty-four lifeboats to be on the ship. But in a rare cost-cutting and space-saving exercise the White Star Line overruled him by deciding that only twenty lifeboats would be carried on the *Titanic*. Carlisle didn't push the matter and the rest, sad to say, is history.

Ship Safety in the North Atlantic (1912) Is Not Ship Safety in the North Atlantic (today)

The *Titanic* disaster led to the convening of the first International Convention for the Safety of Life at Sea (SOLAS) in London, on November 12, 1913. On January 30, 1914, a treaty was signed at the conference that resulted in the formation and worldwide funding of the International Ice Patrol, an agency of the United States Coast Guard that to the present day monitors and reports on the location of North Atlantic icebergs that could pose a threat to transatlantic sea traffic. Over the years, the Coast Guard has experimented with ways of removing dangerous bergs. They've tried gunfire, mines, torpedoes, depth charges, and bombing, but just giving ships early warning so the ice can be avoided has ended up being the most practical solution.

Etcetera

The Brave Postal Workers and Engineers Aboard the Titanic

The *Titanic*'s official name was *RMS Titanic*. RMS stood for Royal Mail Steamer. The ship's official job was to deliver tons of mail to countries on either side of the ocean. The mail was very important because it was one of the few ways of communicating with other people in 1912. The *Titanic* carried over 3,000 mailbags and five postal workers, three Americans and two Brits, on its maiden voyage.

When the *Titanic* hit the iceberg its lower decks began to flood. The postal workers responded by assembling the mail and pulling it to higher decks. They were racing against time, hoping to keep the mail safe until help arrived. Sadly, help never came and the frigid, twenty-eight-degree waters of the North Atlantic claimed them all on the morning of April 15th. The mail was lost as well.

The entire complement of thirty-four engineers and assistant engineers—electricians, plumbers, and boiler room personnel— under the control of Joseph Bell, the Chief Engineer Officer, was also lost when the *Titanic* sank. These brave men kept the power on and the lights burning until almost the very last moment. Their commitment to duty is commemorated in the *Titanic Engineers' Memorial*, which was unveiled in Southampton, England two years after the disaster. (NB: Seventy-eight percent of the *Titanic's* crew went down with the ship.)

The Valiant Musicians Aboard the Ship

The White Star Line hired musicians for the voyage but registered them as second-class passengers so the company could avoid paying union wages. During the sinking, the bandleader, Wallace Hartley led the musicians in playing music, to keep those on board the ship from panicking. Reports from survivors indicate that the band was successful in that mission.

Passengers who were in lifeboats some distance from the *Titanic* could hear, above the tumult and clamor, the orchestra playing lively tunes. Legend has it that Hartley released the musicians only when the incline of the ship made further playing impossible. None of the eight musicians aboard the *Titanic* survived when the great leviathan took its final plunge to the bottom of the ocean.

Sorting Out the Persian Gulf Naming Dispute

It is axiomatic in general semantics that how we label or categorize depends upon our purpose, our projections, and our evaluations; yet the thing labeled does not change just because we change the label or category.[1] Another GS maxim is that words do not have one true meaning: words mean different things to different people; words mean different things at different times; words mean different things in different contexts.[2] Both these dicta, and the GS notion that "the map is not the territory" (words cannot describe all there is to know about anything), are much in evidence in this chapter.

Introduction

On nearly all maps published before 1960, and in most modern-day international treaties, proceedings, and maps, the roughly six hundred-mile-long body of water located between Iran and the Arabian Peninsula is identified by the name *Persian Gulf*. This mirrors conventional practice dating back to first-century ancient Greek geographers. But with the rise of Arab nationalism in the 1960s, a number of Arab countries adopted widespread use of the term *Arab Gulf* or *Arabian Gulf* to refer to this inland sea. Other entities have followed this usage, some of them coming up with additional names, and the result has been a highly contentious dispute over nomenclature involving individuals, nations, global agencies, corporations, universities, and mapmakers.

Some Historical Background

The phrase "Arabian Gulf" (*Sinus Arabicus*) was once used to refer to what is now called the Red Sea. European mapmakers, following the ancient Greek geographers Strabo and Ptolemy among others, went along this usage. Strabo and Ptolemy also utilized the expression *Sinus Persicus* to specify the body of water between the Arabian Peninsula and the Iranian Plateaus. Early Roman historians, in keeping with the traditions of the ancient Greeks, called the waterway "Aquarius Persico."

Persian Muslim geographers, in the early Islamic era and employing Arabic, likewise used the term Persian Sea or Persian Gulf. Most European cartographers, utilizing languages spoken in European countries, have also made use of the name Persian Gulf on their maps.

In 1534, Baghdad was seized by the Ottoman Empire, which gave Turkey access to the port of Basra at the head of the gulf. This event overlapped the early mapmaking efforts of Gerardus Mercator, whose 1541 world globe named the gulf *Sinus Persicus, nunc Mare de Balsera* ("Persian Gulf, now Sea of Basra").[3] On his terrestrial map of 1569, the name was changed to *Mare di Mesendin* (after the Ra's Musandam "the mountaintops" in modern-day Oman).[4]

Mercator's counterpart, the Flemish cartographer Abraham Ortelius, chose the label *Mare El Catif, olim Sinus Persicus* (after the Arabian port of Al Qatif) for his world atlas of 1570.[5] Ortelius also designated the entrance to the gulf *Basora Fretum* (Strait of Basra). Turkey continues to use the term "Gulf of

Basra" today.

In 1840, The London-based *Times Journal*, responding to Iranian objections that England was meddling into Iranian affairs in the Persian Gulf, renamed that body of water the "Britain Sea." That moniker never caught on.

In the 1950s, following the nationalization of the Iranian oil industry, the expulsion of English companies from Iran, and the severing of relations between Iran and England, Roderic Owen, an employee of the Anglo-Iranian Oil Company and an M16 British government officer, published a book titled *The Golden Bubble: Arabian Gulf Documentary.* This book constituted the first literary work of any significance to popularize the term "Arabian Gulf." The tag had originally, and unsuccessfully, been proposed in the 1930s to the British government by Sir Charles Belgrave, a British citizen and advisor to the government of Bahrain.[6]

Diverse Perspectives on a Geographic Label

The Iranian View

Iran employs the term "Persian Gulf" exclusively and does not recognize alternate forms such as the "Arabian Gulf" or "The Gulf." It does not consider the latter term a neutral designation, but sees it as a rebuff to the historical name. Foreign airlines that do not use the phrase "Persian Gulf" on their in-flight monitors are banned from Iran's airspace.[7] The Bushehr province of Iran is the home of Persian Gulf University.

In 2005, Iran proclaimed April 30 "National Persian Gulf Day" (April 30 corresponds with the anniversary of Shah Abbas' successful seventeenth century military campaign, which drove Portugal's navy from the Strait of Hormuz, the narrowest point in the Persian Gulf). This decision was implemented by the High

Council of Cultural Revolution to "counter the attempts of some international institutes and Arabian countries to alter the name of the 'Persian Gulf.'"[8] The Iranian postal service has issued a series of stamps honoring "the national day of Persian Gulf."

In 2006, the top rank of the Iranian soccer league was named the Persian Gulf Cup to advance the Persian label. A few years later, a planned second Islamic Solidarity Games in Iran, originally scheduled to take place in October 2009 and later rescheduled for April 2010, was canceled when the Arab World and Iran could not agree on the use of the term "Persian Gulf" in logos and medals for the Games. Iran's national soccer team does not participate in the Gulf Cup of Nations tournament, which is open to teams from countries that surround gulf waters, due to that competition's name.

(NB: In 1935, Persia's king, Reza Shah, ordered that the name Persia be changed to Iran on all official government offices and embassies. Iran means "land of the Aryans," tribes of whom moved into Iran, India, and Southeast Asia three thousand years ago from Europe. In switching Persia's name to Iran, the king was trying to signal to the world that the population of his country had a different lineage than the populace of Persia's Arab neighbors and a greater affinity with the modern emerging European nations. His plan didn't pan out very well because most people nowadays do not connect the word Iran and Aryan. To make matters worse, people sometimes confuse Iran with Iraq because the names are so similar.)

Arab Views

The following are some arguments that have been made by Arab supporters for the use of the term "Arabian Gulf."

- The name "Persian Gulf" is linked to the Persian Empire that does not exist any more. The Mediterranean Sea used to be called the Roman Sea, and had the Roman Empire lasted, that's what we would call it today.
- The people who live around the gulf are mostly Arabs, so by virtue of demography, it should be called the Arabian Gulf.
- Likewise by virtue of geography: six Arabian countries surround the gulf (Saudi Arabia, Kuwait, Iraq, Bahrain, Qatar, and the United Arab Emirates) compared to one Iran, and they encompass 70 percent of the coastline.

Members of the Arab League, a regional organization of twenty-two member states that have a general goal of promoting the affairs and interests of Arab countries, use the term Arabian Gulf rather than Persian Gulf or The Gulf. There is an Arabian Gulf University in Al-Manamah, Bahrain and an Arabian Gulf Rugby team in Dubai.

The United Nations' View

The United Nations Secretariat on many occasions has directed its staff to use "Persian Gulf" as the sole geographical label for this inland sea.[9] A working paper submitted to the UN Group of Experts on Geographical Names in 2006 stated: "If we were to presume that the sea did not have a name during history, and . . . geographers and specialists were to select a name for this gulf, doubtlessly, they would find no better name than *Persian Gulf* because Iran [Persia] is the largest country adjacent to this water body which possesses the longest coast."[10]

The American View

"Persian Gulf" has been the label sanctioned for US government use since a decision by the State Department's Board of Geographical Names in 1917.[11] The NGA GEOnet Names Server (GNS), which is maintained by the National Geospatial-Intelligence Agency (the official repository of standard spellings of all foreign place names sanctioned by the Board of Geographical Names), lists "Persian Gulf" as the only "conventional" name, along with fourteen unofficial "variants" in different languages, such as "Gulf of Iran," "Gulf of Ajam," "Gulf of Basra," "Arabian Gulf," "Persian-Arabian Gulf," "Gulf of Fars," and "The Gulf."[12]

In recent years, due to increased cooperation with the Arab Persian Gulf states, various branches of the US armed forces have issued orders to their personnel to use the expression "Arabian Gulf" when working in the vicinity, in part to abide by local conventions or simply to follow local laws, like those in the United Arab Emirates (UAE) that prohibit the use of the term "Persian Gulf." For similar reasons, branches of American universities in the area have excised references to "Persian Gulf" in their teaching materials.

Osama bin Laden's View

Following the Iranian Revolution of 1979, there were calls by Ayatollah Khomenei and a number of Islamic groups to use the expression "Islamic Gulf." However, the idea was quickly discarded after Iran was invaded by its mainly Arab and Muslim neighbor, Iraq. The most well-known person who has used the term "Islamic Gulf" in recent times has been Osama bin Laden, who employed the label in a statement he issued on August 23, 1996: "The presence of the USA Crusader military forces on land, sea, and air of the states of the *Islamic Gulf* (italics mine) is the greatest danger threatening the largest oil reserve in the world."[13]

Some Atlas and Media Views

The Associated Press Stylebook 2009 declares: "[Persian Gulf is the] long-established name for the body of water off the southern coast of Iran. Some Arab nations call it the *Arabian Gulf.* Use *Arabian Gulf* only in direct quotations and explain in the text that the body of water is more commonly known as the Persian Gulf."[14]

The National Geographic Society uses the name Persian Gulf in their maps. In 2004, the society published a new edition of its *National Geographic Atlas of the World* using the term "Arabian Gulf" as an alternate name (in smaller type and in parentheses) for "Persian Gulf." This resulted in protests by many Iranians, particularly those in the Internet user community, and led to an Iranian government ban on the distribution of the Society's publications in Iran. On December 30, 2004, the Society reversed its decision and published an *Atlas Update*, removing the parenthetical reference and adding a note: "Historically and most commonly known as the Persian Gulf, this body of water is referred to by some as the Arabian Gulf."[15] The *National Geographic Style Manual* states: The internationally accepted name is Persian Gulf, although Arab countries call the body of water the Arabian Gulf. Where scale permits, National Geographic maps include a map note about the Arabian Gulf. If Arabian Gulf is used in text, it should be explained.[16]

Some atlases and media outlets refer to "The Gulf" without any adjectival qualification. This usage is followed by the BBC, which adopted the practice in the mid 1970s, and *The Times Atlas of the World.* Iran does not consider this an impartial usage but views it as an active contribution to the abandonment of the historical name. In June 2006, Iran banned the sale of *The*

Economist after a map in the magazine omitted "Persian" labeling it just "The Gulf."[17]

The International Hydrographic Organization's View

The International Hydrographic Organization, an international body of eighty member states that provides hydrographic information for worldwide marine navigation and other purposes, uses the name "Gulf of Iran (Persian Gulf)" for this body of water.[18]

Google's View

In early 2008, Google Earth (a virtual globe, map, and geographic information program that was originally called EarthViewer 3D) displayed the names "Persian Gulf" and "Arabian Gulf" next to each other. A subsequent Iranian online petition, harking back to the conventions of pre-1960s mapmakers and the authority of the United Nations, whose official endorsement of the name "Persian Gulf" is based on a small library's worth of archival maps, literary references, and other historical source material, criticized Google for being "unscientific" and unaware of "international standards."[19]

Two months after the "Immediate and Unconditional Deletion" petition went live, Google posted a statement explaining its protocol for naming bodies of water. The statement, which made no direct mention of the Gulf or the Iranian petition, explained that Google decides what to call various geographical features solely by determining what names are in use today. Google Earth "displays the primary, common, local name(s) given to a body of water by the sovereign nations that border it," said Andrew McLaughlin, Google's then director of public policy. "If different countries dispute the proper name for a body of water, our policy is to display both names."[20]

The Google statement also dealt with the idea of the democratization of information. "One of the great features of Google Earth is that it enables us to provide significantly greater amounts of information than flat paper maps," McLaughlin wrote. "It is our fervent hope that different communities will use Google Earth as an open platform to create content that accurately reflects their views."[21]

Some Petitioners' Views

The following are comments from four signatories (participant # 17; 5,636; 995,509; and 1,142,294) to an online petition calling for the "Immediate and Unconditional Deletion of 'Arabian Gulf' from Google Earth." The statements are listed by their rank in the appeal.[22]

How many Jew hating, Christian hating and Iranian hating Sheikhs does it take to pay off these people. The Persian Gulf Arab governments are getting more dangerous by the day and the U.S., Iran, and Israel must stop them! They are the new Nazis of our day and if it was up to them, they would turn all of us into lampshades and bars of soap! Wake up people!

This is absurd. The whole world knows there is no place called Arabian Gulf! Google must be so ignorant or malicious to try to pull off such a stunt.

Historically, what is referred to as "Red Sea" today has been the "Arabian Gulf" because sea voyagers would name a gulf by their destination. So, if I wanted to go to Arabia (which was mostly Jedda and populated coastal towns), I would navigate through "Arabian Gulf" aka

"Red Sea" to get to Arabia. In the old days no one would go to Arabia through Persian Gulf because Arabia was really just the populated cities on or near what is also called "Red Sea" today. If sea voyagers wanted to go to Persia, they would go through "Persian Gulf". These are established naval naming conventions. Please don't politicize this by calling "Persian Gulf" by other names. This naming was employed by Ptolomy [*sic*], the father of geographers since over 2000 years ago. Don't politicize a name and incite millions by calling "Persian Gulf" by any other name. If Arabs like the name "Arabian Gulf" so much, why don't they call the "Red Sea" by its true name, "Arabian Gulf"? It is confusing to call 2 different Gulfs by the same name.

This has always been Persian Gulf. Through history and all maps it is indicated as Persian Gulf. There is no reason to change its name now unless for a political reason.

PART 4

Practical Wisdom from Notable Thinkers

Alfred Schweitzer and Albert Korzybski: Champions of Humanity

Albert Schweitzer (1875–1965) and Alfred Korzybski (1879–1950) were European-born contemporaries with powerful and wide-ranging intellects who devoted themselves to alleviating human suffering and advancing human welfare. Both men believed in a unity of idealism and realism and both practiced what they preached.

Schweitzer, like Korzybski, was a polymath. He not only studied but mastered philosophy, music, theology, and medicine. He also became the world's authority on Bach and organ building. At the age of thirty, he went to medical school and devoted the majority of his life to relieving the suffering of the people of Central Africa while still staying current on the affairs of the world and providing commentary on ethics, war, nuclear weapons, and environmental degradation. In 1952, he was awarded the Nobel Peace Prize.

Korzybski studied engineering, mathematics, and philosophy. As a child, he was fluent in four languages. In 1933, he published his magnum opus, *Science and Sanity*, which details the basic formulations of general semantics (GS), a non-Aristotelian system for improved human evaluation. His system has had significant influence in helping people to become more effective, accurate, and discriminating in their communications

144

with others and with themselves. GS has also positively impacted disciplines such as Rational-Emotive Behavior Therapy (REBT), Neurolinguistic Programming (NLP), Media Ecology, and speech and language education.

Schweitzer and Korzybski were deeply affected by World War I. Schweitzer lost his mother in the conflict and served as a prisoner of war. During the time he stayed in prison camps, he worked on *The Philosophy of Civilization*, which was first published in two parts in 1923. In that book he presents his "Reverence for Life" philosophy, which will be discussed in more detail later.

Korzybski served in the Russian army during World War I. Wounded several times on the battlefield, he intensely felt the distress of others in the hostilities. War assignments eventually took him to the United States where he learned English and published *Manhood of Humanity*, a book that discusses what makes humans human and his theory of "time-binding."

Schweitzer's Philosophy of Civilization

I want to be the pioneer of a new Renaissance. I want to throw faith in a new humanity, like a burning torch into our dark times.
–Albert Schweitzer, *Civilization and Ethics*

Schweitzer characterized civilization as the quest for spiritual and material progress in all spheres of life, accompanied by the ethical development of individuals and humankind.[1] He observed that the Roman Stoics (e.g., Seneca, Epictetus, and Marcus Aurelius) set a baseline for such ethical development in that they advised being present in the world and facing one's problems. Schweitzer believed theirs was a more constructive and humane approach to life than the pessimistic view of philosophers such as

Schopenhauer and certain religions, which harp on a negation of the world and passively submitting to fate.

Like NYU Professor Neil Postman, the author of *Building a Bridge to the Eighteenth Century*, Schweitzer was partial to the eighteenth-century Enlightenment values of reason and concern for civilizaticn. He argued that those ideals became moribund in the nineteenth century, as people became lost in the nonessential, conforming to a mind-numbing compliance with Machine Age living conditions. Such circumstances made it difficult for a system of mcrality to progress.

In 1923, Schweitzer put forth his system of ethics and a comprehensive worldview in *The Philosophy of Civilization*. In that book, he discusses his "Reverence for Life" philosophy, which involves the notion that one can achieve spiritual harmony in life by accepting reality, working to the best of one's ability, and being ethical.

Schweitzer's Reverence for Life Philosophy begins with the idea that all life, including that of plants and animals, is precious. In his autobiography he illustrates that premise with the following story:[2]

When working in Africa, Schweitzer bought from some villagers a young osprey they had caught on a sandbank, in order to rescue it from their cruel machinations. But then he had to decide whether to let it starve, or kill a number of small fishes every day to keep it alive. He chose the latter course, but every day the responsibility to sacrifice one life for another caused him pain.

Schweitzer noted that all human beings who possess a will to live are faced with the dilemma of having to destroy life in order to survive. But if one subscribes to the reverence for life ethic, a person only injures and takes life under a necessity he cannot avoid, and never from thoughtlessness.

Schweitzer, like Korzybski, stressed the notion that to achieve a measure of contentment one should work hard at achieving one's goals and not set unrealistic expectations. To keep expectations "real," he advised carefully assessing them. For example, Schweitzer decided at age thirty to enter medical school so he could qualify as a doctor and go to Africa to minister to the poor. Although many of his friends advised him that this was a highly impractical plan, Schweitzer thought differently: "I held the venture to be justified, because I had considered it for a long time and from every point of view, and I thought that I had good health, sound nerves, energy, practical common sense, toughness, prudence, very few wants, and everything else that might be necessary for the pursuit of my idea. I believed, further, that I had the inner fortitude to endure any eventual failure of my plan."[3] Without these compensating factors, Schweitzer says he would not have undertaken such a daunting enterprise.

Schweitzer believed in the importance of being involved in life. He had little use for religions and belief systems that promoted states of nonbeing or surrendering to circumstances. Ancient Greek thinking (which led to resignation) and Middle Ages Christianity (with its focus on the hereafter rather than on the here and now) were anathema to him. The Renaissance, which brought with it freedom from the medieval rejection of the world and paved the path to the Enlightenment, was far more to his taste.

Schweitzer, like Korzybski, contended that for humanity to progress, people need to use their power of reason to battle mindless conformity. He asserted such conformity is urged upon us by "The organized political, social, and religious associations of our time [who] are at work convincing the individual not to develop his convictions through his own thinking but to assimilate the ideas they present to him. Any man who thinks for himself is to them inconvenient and even ominous. He does not offer sufficient guarantee that he will merge into the organization."[4] To battle "authoritarian truth," Schweitzer asserted there needs to be a "rekindling of the fire of thought."

According to Schweitzer, one doesn't have to undertake exceptional tasks to serve humanity. He states "We can all find grace if we seize the chance to act humanly toward those who need another human being. In this way we serve both the spiritual and the good. Nothing can keep us from the . . . job of direct human service. So many opportunities are missed because we let them pass by."[5]

Kozybski's Science of Man

'Tis time new hopes should animate mankind,
New light should dawn...
–Robert Browning, *Paracelsus*

This quotation from Browning was chosen by Korzybski to begin the new introduction he was preparing for the second edition of *Manhood of Humanity*. He died before that introduction could be finished, but in his talks and writings, he followed Browning's admonition to bring new hope and light to animate mankind.

In 1921, Korzybski published his first book, *Manhood of Humanity*, which discusses the science and art of "Human Engineering" (twelve years later, in his second book, *Science and Sanity*, he relabeled his system General Semantics). By that term, he meant the science and art of directing the energies and capacities of individuals to the expansion of human wellbeing. He argued such a system needed to be founded on established facts: "it must accord with what is *characteristic* of Man—it must be based upon a right conception of what Man is—upon a right understanding of Man's place in the scheme of Nature."⁶

What is Man? Korzybski asserted that two basic responses have been provided to answer this question through the course of history—one biological (man is an animal, a certain kind of animal) and the other a mixture, partly biological and partly mythological or partly biological and partly philosophical (man is a combination or union of animal with something supernatural). Korzybski proposed a third reply that he predicated on the notion that human beings possess, in varying degrees, a natural faculty that gives them dignity as people and separates them from other forms of life. He called this faculty the *time-binding* power or *time-binding* capacity and said men, women, and children constitute the time-binding class of life.

Time-binding, the capacity to transmit knowledge across time, can be accomplished only by a class of life that employs symbols (language, numbers, etc.) as a means for communication. Through using their time-binding potential, human beings have gone from living in caves to residing in high-rise apartments, from getting around on foot to zipping along in automobiles, from obtaining food that is nearby to being able to acquire fare from all over the world. Meanwhile, the rest of the animal kingdom, a class of life Korzybski labeled *space-binders* because animals transform energy through movement in space, do things pretty much the way they have always done them through the centuries.

Korzybski noted that the scientific method has been an exceptionally valuable time-binding tool, as it has enabled humanity to make great technological strides. This method allows scientists the freedom to revise their fundamental assumptions, terminologies, and undefined terms (which involve hidden assumptions) and, as a consequence, come up with reliable and predictable outcomes. Korzybski argued that extending the scientific method to the problems of everyday life would generate similar constructive results.

To move humanity forward, he also recommended that people become aware of how our language structure influences the way we think about and perceive the world and ourselves. For example, science tells us we live in a process world where everything is in flux. But our language structure can fool us into thinking reality is static and immobile (e.g., He is tall, She is good, They are bad). Our language structure also pushes us to think in either-or terms (e.g., good-bad, old-young, wrong-weak, big-little), a type of thought that compels us to reflect in extremes rather than in *degrees*. Wendell Johnson, one of Korzybski's disciples, noted that using either-or choices to set goals (e.g., I must be popular, strong, attractive) can result in a disorder he labeled the *IFD disease* (going from Idealization to Frustration to Demoralization).[7]

Korzybski observed that when we use words, we abstract (we select, we leave out things). Knowing we abstract can help us to become more conscious of the possibilities of miscommunication, as we can only "see" in part and "know" in part. Because we are imperfect receivers and transmitters of what is going on in the world, Korzybski continually emphasized in his writings that accurate communication, with ourselves and with others, is a highly complex task. The following are some formulations he devised to overcome communication barriers:

- *Adopt a "to me" attitude*: There is considerable variation in the way we sense things, the way we react, and the way we symbolize.

- *Delay your reaction*: A delay of even a fraction of a section permits the nervous system to consider alternatives.
- *Indexing*: A reminder that no two things are identical: teacher$_1$ is not teacher$_2$, car$_1$ is not car$_2$.
- *Dating*: A reminder that no one thing is ever the same twice: Bill (today) is not Bill (yesterday), Iraq (2002) is not Iraq (2012).
- *Etc.*: A reminder that you can not say all, or know all, about anything.

Conclusion

Schweitzer's worldview was based on his idea of *Reverence for Life*, which he thought was his greatest single contribution to humankind. This outlook was premised on the notion that Western civilization was in decay because of gradually abandoning its ethical foundations—those of affirming life. He also consistently emphasized the necessity to think, rather than merely act on the basis of fleeting impulses or by follow prevailing opinion, as the only way individuals and humanity as a whole could progress.

Korzybski posited that human beings are limited in what they know by the structure of their nervous systems and the structure of their languages. His GS system included modifying the way we approach the world, for example, with an attitude of "I don't know; let's see," to better discern "reality" as shown by modern science. He emphasized that in life, the map is not the territory: people's beliefs about reality and their awareness of things ("the map") are not reality itself or everything they could be aware of ("the territory"). He believed his system would help people, and humankind in general, maximize their potential.

Schweitzer and Korzybski, in their work and their lives, understood that human nature is not intractable and undergirded by selfishness and greed, and with hard work and determination, individuals, and by extension societies, can progress morally and materially. Their respective philosophies, Reverence for Life and general semantics, were largely envisioned to help people and cultures realize those objectives.

13

How Science Should Be Done: Insights from Santiago Ramón y Cajal

General semantics advocates a scientific approach for making effective evaluations. Such an approach has enabled humankind to go from living in caves to living in high-rise apartment buildings, to go from traveling by foot to traveling by supersonic jet, and to go from having leeches applied to one's body to heal illnesses to having modern medicines do that job. It's hard to argue that, for the most part, science has been a huge boon to humanity.

Spanish physician and Nobel laureate Santiago Ramón y Cajal (1852–1934) made important contributions to science. A seminal figure in the field of neuroanatomy, Cajal was the first scientist to show that the central nervous system consists of individual neurons that typically conduct information in one direction. He discovered the synapse and went on to describe the organization of all major neural systems as chains of independent neurons. And he was the first person to explain in modern terms the organization of reflex and voluntary control pathways to the motor system. (He also made several lasting contributions to Spanish literature—his autobiography, a popular book of aphorisms, and reflections on old age.)

In addition to leaving a legacy of outstanding scientific research, Cajal published a book, *Advice for a Young Investigator*,

153

that sought to educate the novice scientist about how science was done and how Cajal believed it should be done. This still relevant anecdotal guide, which was retranslated and published in 1999 by MIT Press, offers valuable information and advice not only for new investigators, but also for seasoned professionals and individuals who are simply interested in science. Some of that knowledge, arranged in section-order from the introduction and nine chapters of the book, will now be presented.

Advice for a Young Investigator

Introduction

In the book's first chapter, Cajal talks about science as a superior form of human evaluating and the limitations of subjective reasoning. "The history of civilization proves beyond doubt just how sterile the repeated attempts of metaphysics to guess at nature's laws have been. Instead, there is every reason to believe that when the human intellect ignores reality and concentrates within, it can no longer explain the simplest inner workings of life's machinery or of the world around us."[1]

Cajal argues that science cannot hope to understand ultimate causes. "Our brain is an organ of action that is directed toward practical tasks; it does not appear to have been built for discovering the ultimate causes of things, but rather for determining their immediate causes and invariant relationships. And whereas this may appear in fact to be very little, it is in fact a great deal. Having been granted the immense advantage of participating in the unfolding of our world, and of modifying it to life's advantage, we may proceed quite nicely without knowing the essence of things."[2]

Cajal observes that scientists who make great contributions to their fields do so by not just applying their intellect. They also exhibit great perseverance and motivation. "I believe that all outstanding work in art as well as science, results from immense zeal applied to a great idea."[3]

Beginner's Traps

Cajal warns that undue admiration for authority stifles initiative and prevents the formulation of original scientific work. Another debilitating notion is to think the most important problems are already solved. "Nature offers inexhaustible wealth to all. There is no reason to envy our predecessors, or to exclaim with Alexander following the victories of Philip, 'My father is going to leave me nothing to conquer!'"[4] And, there are no small problems in science. Cajal declares, "Problems that appear small are large problems that are not understood. Instead of tiny details unworthy of the intellectual, we have men whose tiny intellects cannot rise to penetrate the infinitesimal."[5]

Cajal maintains that it is important to fight the false distinction between *theoretical science* and *applied science*, with accompanying praise for the latter and deprecation of the former. "Does anyone lack the common sense to understand that applications derive immediately from the discovery of fundamental principles and new data? In Germany, France, and England the factory and laboratory are closely intertwined, and very often the scientist himself . . . directs its industrial application."[6]

To succeed in laboratory science one does not have to be a genius. The important thing, according to Cajal, is to focus one's energies and to keep at it: "in scientific undertakings the *slow* prove to be as useful as the fast because scientists like artists are judged by the quality of what they produce, not by the speed of production. I would even venture to add that as a very common compensation *slow* brains have great endurance for prolonged concentration."[7]

Intellectual Qualities

"Indispensable qualities for the research worker include independent judgment, intellectual curiosity, perseverance, devotion to country, and a burning desire for reputation."[8]

When it comes to gaining reputation, Cajal notes, "It is certainly true that the scientist's fame is not as great as the playwright or artist's glamour and popularity. People live in a world of sentiment, and it is asking too much of them to provide warmth and support for the heroes of reason. Nevertheless, scholars do have their public. It consists of the intellectual aristocracy that dwells in every country, speaks every language, and reaches the most distant of future generations."[9]

On the topic of "scientific originality," Cajal states, "The drive to carry out great undertakings may certainly come from the inducements of patriotism and a lofty desire for reputation. Nevertheless, our novice runs the risk of failure without additional traits: a strong inclination toward originality, a taste for research, and a desire to experience the incomparable gratification associated with the act of discovery itself.[10] . . . As we have already noted, the joyful emotion associated with the act of discovery is so great that it is easy to understand the sublime madness of Archimedes."[11]

What Newcomers to Biological Research Should Know

"We may learn a great deal from books, but we learn much more from the contemplation of nature—the reason and occasion for all books. The direct examination of phenomena has an indescribably disturbing and leavening effect on our mental inertia—a certain exciting and revitalizing quality altogether absent, or barely perceptible, in even the most faithful copies and descriptions of reality."[12]

Cajal believes labeling is especially important in scientific discovery. "Discovery is often a matter of simply fitting a piece of data to a law, or wrapping it in a broader theoretical framework, or, finally classifying it. Thus, it may be concluded that to discover is to name something correctly, something that had been christened incorrectly or conditionally before . . . A well-chosen word can save an enormous amount of thought, because to *name* is to classify, to establish ideal affiliations—analogous relationships—between little-known phenomena, and to identify the general idea or principle wherein in they lie latent, like the tree within its seed."[13]

For investigators confused about what problem to work on, Cajal offers the following suggestion: "when we discover ourselves surrounded by a number of equally promising and fertile problems to work on, choose the one whose methodology we understand clearly, and the one we have a decided liking for. This is the good advice Darwin used to give his students when they asked for a problem to work on. The rationale for this approach is that our intellect redoubles its efforts when perceiving the reward of pleasure or utility in the distance."[14]

Diseases of the Will

Cajal avows that scientific investigators should attempt original work and write about it. He is intolerant of excuses. "We have all seen teachers who are wonderfully talented and full of energy and initiative—with ample facilities at their disposal—who never produce any original work and almost never write anything. Their students and admirers wait anxiously for the masterpiece worthy of the lofty opinion they have formed of their teacher. But the great work is never written, and the teacher remains silent . . . such teachers suffer from a disease of the will."[15]

Cajal goes on to say, "We render a tribute of respect to those who add original work to a library, and withhold it from those who carry a library around in their head. If one is to become a mere phonograph, it is hardly worth the effort of complicating cerebral organization with study and reflection. Our neurons must be used for more substantial things. Not only to know but also to transform knowledge; not only to experience but also to construct—this is the standard for the genuine man of science to follow."[16]

Cajal counsels novice investigators that, "a scholar's positive contribution is measured by the sum of the original data that he contributes. Hypotheses come and go, but data remain. Theories desert us, while data defend us. They are our true resources, our real estate, and our best pedigree."[17]

Social Factors Beneficial to Scientific Work

Cajal argues that the state and universities should support scientific investigators. "Government and educational institutions must contribute to the formation and cultivation of these laboratory patriots by creating a nurturing social environment for them, and by freeing them, insofar as possible, from the preoccupations of material existence."[18]

He also maintains that scientific progress can be made in the absence of optimal material conditions: "Enthusiasm and perseverance work miracles."[19]

Cajal's view on marriage is quite dated, but a hundred years ago—when men were the primary scientific investigators—it might have spurred some reluctant researchers to the altar: "[A scientific investigator] will not emulate the selfishness of Epicurus, who did not marry in an attempt to avoid cares and woes, nor the exaggerated refinement of Napoleon, whose only use for a woman was a nurse in old age. For the man of science the aid of a wife is just as necessary in youth as in old age. A woman at one's side may be likened to a knapsack in battle: without the accessory one fights unencumbered, but after the battle, then what?"[20]

Stages of Scientific Research

Cajal on *scientific observation*: "Perez de Ayala has stated it very wisely and skillfully: 'Look at things as if for the very first time.' That is, admire them afresh, disregarding what we remember from books, stilted description, and conventional wisdom. We must free our minds of prejudice and fading images, and make a definite point to see and judge for ourselves, as if the object had been created for the gratification and delight of our intellect alone. In short, we must re-create, insofar as possible, the state of mind of the fortunate scholar who discovered the fact under consideration, or who first stated the problem—a blend of surprise, emotion, and lively curiosity."[21]

Cajal on *hypotheses*: "One shouldn't need reminding that all great investigators have been prolific hypothesis generators. It has been said with deep conviction that hypotheses are the first murmurings of reason in the darkness of the unknown; the sounding instrument lowered into the mysterious abyss; in short, the high, lofty, and audacious bridge connecting the familiar shore with the unexplored continent."[22]

Cajal on *proof*: "Once a hypothesis is clearly formulated, it must be submitted to the ratification of testing. For this, we must choose experiments or observations that are precise, complete, and conclusive. One of the characteristic attributes of a great intellect is the ability to design appropriate experiments. They immediately find ways of solving problems that average scholars only clarify with long and exhausting investigation."[23]

On Writing Scientific Papers

"Mr. Billings is a scholarly Washington librarian who is burdened by the task of classifying thousands of publications where essentially the same facts are presented in different ways, or truths known since antiquity are expounded upon. He counsels scientific writers to govern themselves by the following rules: (1) Have something to say, (2) say it, (3) stop once it is said, and (4) give the article a suitable title and order of presentation."[24]

Cajal cautions the novice investigator about how to respond to unjust attacks: "When unjustly attacked and forced to defend ourselves, let us do so nobly. Unsheathe your sword, but with tip blunted—adorned with a bouquet of flowers, to use a common phrase. It is painful to admit that in the majority of cases the objectors are defending their own infallibility rather than a doctrine or principle. Eucken very aptly notes that under the pretext of refuting principles, 'everyone defends himself in his own way and according to his nature . . . It is the instinct of self-preservation that reacts.'"[25]

With regard to writing style, Cajal states, "the style of our work should be genuine, didactic, sober, simple, and free of affectation, and it should reveal a preoccupation with order and clarity. Undue emphasis, oratory, and hyperbole should never enter into purely scientific writing, unless we wish to forfeit the confidence of scholars, who will come to regard us as dreamers or poets, incapable of studying and applying cold logic to a problem."[26]

The Investigator as Teacher

"It is well known that youth show their respect for famous men by imitating them. Therefore, it would be a worthwhile contribution to the education of the will if each and every teacher would recount with genuine affection, and with the deliberate intent of suggestion, the anecdotal and more formal biographies of the scientists who have distinguished themselves most in the development of the student's chosen field."[27]

Cajal maintains that science teachers should convey to their students a sense of mission and optimism. "We have already stated that a master worthy of the name must always convey to his pupils the idea that science is in a perpetual state of flux, that it progresses and grows continuously, and that we can all contribute a grain of sand to the imposing monument of progress if we truly resolve to do so."[28]

Finally, Cajal believes good science teachers should motivate students to take on challenging tasks that may bring the student greater honors than the teacher. "When the beginner can finally walk alone, attempts should be made to infuse him with an appreciation of originality . . . The greatest honor that can come to the master does not lie in molding students to follow him, but in producing scholars who will surpass him."[29]

GS Wisdom from Wendell Johnson

Wendell Johnson had a great gift for making general semantics clear and compelling. That gift is particularly evident in his book *Your Most Enchanted Listener*. Between its covers, one finds elegant writing and excellent examples that illustrate the practicality of general semantics to everyday life.

The front flap of the 1956 Harper edition of *Your Most Enchanted Listener* offers the following description: "This book might well be called *How to Talk to Yourself,* because it is fundamentally concerned with knowing what you're saying and saying what you mean. It is also a book about how to be dependable as an observer and honest as a reporter. It is about how not to tell a lie. It is about how not to be a sucker." Sound intriguing? Let's look into the manuscript and see what else can be discovered there.

Your Most Enchanted Listener

In a chapter titled "Four Hundred Little Tugs Each Day," Johnson observes that the average four-year-old asks four hundred questions a day. These hundreds of questions are like tiny ropes at which the child tugs unremittingly in a heroic effort to get the world inside his head. And "The fateful fact is that he does get the world inside his head—*a* world that is his. And it is the world in which he is to spend the rest of his life—unless he turns out to be one of those rare creative persons who retain a country boy's popeyed view of the commonplace."[1]

Commenting on another aspect of human development, Johnson notes that unlike other animals, humans are "specialists in not specializing." Because of our highly developed brain cortex we have become the most adaptable creature in the world. People live all over the planet and perform a multiplicity of tasks. And one thing we are particularly good at doing is manipulating symbols, particularly language.

In our use of language, Johnson maintains that no matter whom one is talking to, every speaker is his most beguiled listener. In silent thoughts or speaking outwardly, we are always talking to ourselves. That being the case, he advises that we should listen carefully to what we tell ourselves day after day, as our thoughts are profound influencers of our emotions and actions.

Johnson says paying attention to our thoughts can increase the possibilities for clear thinking and good will toward others, two key elements necessary to human progress. He particularly recommends the use of the scientific method—question, observe, report, conclude—as an aid to improve clear thinking, and notes that framing "useful questions" is of particular importance in that enterprise. (The most sharply defining feature of such questions is they are the kind that can be answered directly or indirectly by means of factual information that can be obtained now, or conceivably in the future, or that has been obtained by making observations.)

In further expounding on the scientific method, Johnson asserts, "The one form of human behavior that is consistently honest by conscious design is that behavior which is scientific. If one really believes honesty is the best policy, then one will strive to behave as scientifically as possible. If you try it you may decide against it, but then at least you will know that you prefer dishonesty . . . truth tends to change as the restless atoms weave anew and anew the shimmering fabric of fact. Error, on the other hand, agreed upon and firmly fixed in legend and in law, is something one can count on from day to day, even from century to century."[2]

Johnson declares we can also count on the fact that what we see in life is determined not alone by what stares us in the face, but also by our wishes and our doubts, our likes and dislikes, our fears, assumptions, knowledge, and ignorance. Other people may not view things the way we view them because we don't all share the same projections.

When we speak about the world as we observe it, we talk largely about our feelings about it or our judgments of it. "We do not often *describe* things, persons, and events; we more commonly *evaluate* them as beautiful or good, wise or stupid, ugly or bad. Such words, of course, describe nothing. They express our personal standards and reflect our feelings of whatever we may be responding to."[3]

Johnson further says, "the worlds that we manage to get inside our heads are mostly worlds of words, words that become our unrelenting own. And so it is that in these worlds of words inside our heads we hold ourselves captive. To a far greater degree than we are prompted to suppose we do, we take our words to be reality, and by so much we lose contact with the world outside the bony brain cases from which we peer nearly unsightfully."[4]

Individuals who claim to know *all* about people or things are particularly "unsightful" with regard to how much a person can know, as one of the most tantalizing truths in life is that there is very much we shall never know. There's simply too much information around for a person to take all of it in completely, and our senses are not developed enough to capture everything that is happening in our environments. On these two basic facts, Johnson says, rests the conviction that humility is a vital part of wisdom.

Johnson cautions that we can be fooled into thinking our words describe *factual* truths. This can occur if one consults a dictionary with the assumption that the definition of a term contained in the dictionary describes the word's true meaning. But a dictionary is no more than a catalog of symbolic inventions. A definition is a *formal* truth, and as such, it should not be mistaken for a factual proposition. A definition is not a statement about the nonverbal world of fact and experience. It is words about words.

Labeling by means of categories is another circumstance that involves words about words. Such classifying should be done with careful consideration, as individual occurrences in the "real world" may not conform to broad generalization. Johnson states, "Any statement made about a *category*—the category 'professor,' for example—amounts to a definition, and it fits any particular member of the category, any particular professor, for example, only partially at best. It is very useful indeed to distinguish clearly between verbal definitions, which are words about words, and factual statements, which are words about things that are not-words."[5]

Johnson notes that general semantics can help us to become more sensitive to the way language influences thought and action and can help us to become more aware of the pitfalls and shortcomings of everyday linguistic conventions through "a consciousness of abstracting and of all that abstracting tends to involve: identification of words and things, of the seeable and unseeable; projection; overdefinition and underdefinition of terms; the multiordinality of abstracting; and all the rest of what he [Korzybski] summarized and organized in that curious three-dimensional diagram of his that he called the structural differential."[6]

A central tenet of GS is the notion that experience is complex: "we usually say—because the prevailing forms of our language say it for us—that one thing affects another, that A affects B, as though B also did not affect A. In the meantime, A and B interact in practically all instances. The way we feel affects what and how much we eat and what and how much we eat affects the way we feel. Action leads to reaction as dependably as the sun rides the heavens day after day. We take for granted that structure determines function, but the biceps of any weight-lifter are arresting evidence of the effect that function has on structure. The thought affects the thinker. And the poet Yeats etched it memorably: 'How can we tell the dancer from the dance?'"[7]

In discussing self-reflexive relationships, Johnson says, "Much that is of the greatest significance to us in all this business about the ways we talk about—and the ways we understand—relationships is to be pointed up especially with the connection with what we may call self-reflexive relationships. These involve a kind of recoil or feedback, as seen in the thinker on the effects of his own thoughts, on the observer of his own observations, on the dreamer of his own dreaming—and remembering Yeats, the effects on the dancer of the dance."[8]

A particularly important kind of self-reflexive relationship entails the idea that any speaker is his own listener, often his most responsive and vulnerable listener. "[But] Our common language tends to strongly obscure this fact. It is only by taking special pains—by carrying out a personal language reform, no less—that one can talk about it in anything less than an effective fashion. In our usual way we talk about the speaker and the listener as though they were two different persons, not as though they were one and the same individual. It is not to be missed or passed over lightly that in English we have no word for a-speaker-listening-to-and-being-affected-by-and-responding-to-himself. About the nearest we ever come to referring to this universally occurring and impressively ignored phenomenon is found in the phrase that only partially covers it: a man talking to himself."[9]

Feedback processes provide striking examples of self-reflexiveness and self-reflexive relationships. A fairly practical way to approach this formulation is to recognize two general kinds of feedback: internal and external. The former is at play in the speaker who is being reflexive about something he has just said, while external feedback is operating when the speaker is being sensitive to the reactions of other people to what he has said.

The importance of all this to each of us arises particularly from the fact that in our attempt to talk about reality we do two things with language: we point verbally to individual facts, and having done that, we arrange and organize them; we make statements about the relationships among them. "Gearing ourselves to reality appears to be in large measure a matter of becoming more and more sensitive to such relationships, more adroit in recognizing them, and more effective in talking and thinking about them . . . the more we do this the more freedom we come by, freedom *from* what Stuart Chase recognized as the tyranny of words, freedom *to* evaluate our own evaluations and so self-reflexively to work our way, however slowly, toward the higher reaches of what might have been."[10]

After being a bystander in two hundred meetings of boards and committees, Irving J. Lee, the author of the general semantics classic *How to Talk with People*, reported that the major types of trouble people have in trying to talk with each other all reflect in one way or another on the jamming of feedback.

Remarking on Lee's findings, Johnson says, "People seem to be far more powerfully driven to talk at each other than listen to each other, and when they do listen the kind of feedback they give the speaker—and the kind of reaction the speaker makes, in turn, to this feedback—appears distressingly often to be self-defensive and generally competitive, or insincere and thus misleading, rather than clarifying, honest and co-operative."[11]

"What makes this problem so intriguing is that as a matter of objective fact nothing passes from speaker to listener except air waves and light waves and, as such, as manifestations of physical force, they are impressively weak! . . . [yet] these really feeble waves commonly disturb the cardiovascular system, endocrine glands, autonomic nervous system, skeletal musculature, even the digestive system of the listener, with effects ranging all the way from increased heart rate and blanching of the skin to regurgitation and even loss of consciousness . . . Meanwhile nothing except the gentlest vibrations in the air and perfectly harmless reflections of light passes between speaker and listener— even when the speaker shouts, trembles, jumps up and down quite violently. An effective awareness of this should go far to make listeners less fearful and speakers less confident of the threatening powers of words, particularly snarled or shouted words, as such."[12]

Johnson argues that as listeners we might minimize our feelings of being threatened by maintaining the clearest possible awareness of our own projecting. "It helps also to do whatever might be feasible to check with the speaker in order to determine whether any such feelings as we may have at any time are justified, so far, at least, as the speaker's intentions are concerned. Within limits, we can as speakers reduce our listeners' feelings of being threatened simply by being alert to any possible manifestations of such feelings on their part, and by providing reassurances when they are called for, even if they are not asked for."[13] That is sage counsel from a book overflowing with such advice.

Notes

Chapter 1. People in Quandaries: The Semantics of Personal Adjustment

1. Wendell Johnson, *People in Quandaries: The Semantics of Personal Adjustment* (Concord, CA: International Society for General Semantics, 2002), vii.
2. Ibid., 13.
3. Ibid., 11.
4. Ibid., 17.
5. Ibid., 28.
6. Ibid., 33–34.
7. Ibid., 47–48.
8. Ibid., 48.
9. Ibid., 58.
10. Ibid., 68.
11. Ibid., 82–83.
12. Ibid., 95.
13. Ibid., 92.
14. Ibid., 112–113.
15. Ibid., 113.
16. Ibid., 119–120.
17. Ibid., 145.
18. Ibid., 161.
19. Ibid., 251–252.
20. Ibid., 262.
21. Ibid., 268.
22. Ibid., 282.
23. Ibid., 292–293.
24. Ibid., 350.
25. Ibid., 365.

26. Ibid., 386.
27. Ibid., 382–383.

Chapter 2. How We Defeat Ourselves by the Way We Talk—And What to Do About It

1. Neil Postman, *Crazy Talk, Stupid Talk: How We Defeat Ourselves by the Way We Talk—and What to Do About It* (New York: Delacorte, 1976), xi.
2. Ibid., xi–xii.
3. Ibid., 26.
4. Ibid., 139.
5. Ibid., 256.
6. Ibid., 256.
7. Ibid., 258.

Chapter 3. Over/Under-Defined Terms in American Politics

1. Alfred Korzybski. *Science and Sanity,* 5th ed. (Englewood, NJ: Institute of General Semantics, 1994), lxiv.

2. The arguments presented in this section are more fully developed in Leonard R. N. Ashley, "Bordering on the Impossible," *ETC: A Review of General Semantics* 61, no. 2 (April 2004): 343–348.

3. This section was originally published in a slightly different form in Martin H. Levinson, "Democracy Here is Not Necessarily Democracy There," *ETC: A Review of General Semantics* 63, no. 2 (April 2006): 215–216.

4. Helen Nowlis, *Drugs Demystified* (Paris, UNESCO, 1975), 12.

Chapter 4. Science Versus Religion: A False Dichotomy

1. Additional information on the sections in this chapter can be found in Lawrence M. Principe, *Science and Religion*, DVD, (Chantilly, VA: The Teaching Company, 2006).

Chapter 5. Practical GS Applications

1. Rachel Lauer, "General Semantics and the Future of Education," *ETC: A Review of General Semantics* 24, no. 4 (1965–66): 401.

2. Francis P. Chisholm, *Introductory Lectures on General Semantics* (Lakeville, CT: Institute of General Semantics, 1956), iii–iv.

3. John C. Merrill, *Journalism Ethics: Philosophical Foundations for News Media* (New York: St. Martin's Press, 1997), 155.

4. Bruce I. Kodish, "Psycho-Logical Fate and Freedom," *ETC: A Review of General Semantics* 62, no. 4 (October 2005): 360.

5. Michael Cole, "Message from the Dr. Sanford I. Berman Chair in General Semantics," *Department of Communication, University of San Diego*, accessed August 18, 2012, http://communication.ucsd.edu/berman/.

6. Terence P. Moran, "Media Ecology is General Semantics Writ Large," *General Semantics Bulletin* 74/75 (2007/2008): 38.

7. Eleanor Parkhurst, "Some Implications of General Semantics Methodology for Social Work," *ETC: A Review of General Semantics* 61, no. 4 (December 2004): 641.

8. Ibid., 648.

9. William Exton Jr., "Managerial Judgment and Critical Thinking," in *Thinking Creatically*, ed. Kenneth G. Johnson (Englewood, NJ: Institute of General Semantics), 33.

10. Wilson J. Bentley, "General Semantics for Engineers?!," *ETC: A Review of General Semantics* 26, no. 1 (March 1969): 64.

11. Ibid., 68.

12. Sixten E. Flach, "General Semantics in Technical Assistance Work," *ETC: A Review of General Semantics* 24, no. 3 (September 1967): 335.

13. Alfred Korzybski, "General Semantics, Psychiatry, Psychotherapy and Prevention," in *General Semantics in Psychotherapy*, eds. Isabel Caro and Charlotte Schuchardt Read (Brooklyn, NY: Institute of General Semantics, 2003), 36.

14. Gerard I. Nierenberg, *The Complete Negotiator* (New York: Nierenberg & Zeif, 1986), 255.

15. Frank Scardilli, "How Just is Our System of Justice?," presentation at the "Across the Generations Conference: Legacies of Hope and Meaning," New York, September 13, 2009.

16. John Magee, *The General Semantics of Wall Street* (Springfield, MA: John Magee, 1958), 1.

17. Linda Anstendig, "Building Critical Thinking Into a Freshman Writing Course," in Johnson, *Thinking Creatically*, 211.

18. Alvin M. Weinberg, "General Semantics and the Teaching of Physics," *The American Physics Teacher* 7, no. 2 (April 1939): 104.

19. Martin H. Levinson, "Using GS to Enhance Organizational Leadership," *ETC: A Review of General Semantics* 62, no. 3 (July 2005): 251.

20. Ibid., 259.

21. Milton Dawes, "General Semantics Guides Toward Better Futures," *General Semantics Bulletin* 74/75 (2007/2008): 84.

22. Nicholas Johnson, *What Do You Mean and How Do You Know?* (Morrisville, NC: Lulu Press, 2009), 8.

23. Bronislaw Malinowski, testimonial comment in *Science and Sanity: An Introduction to Non-Aristotelian Systems and General Semantics*, 5th ed., Alfred Korzybski (Englewood, NJ: Institute of General Semantics, 1994), 784.

24. William J. Williams, *General Semantics and the Social Sciences* (New York: Philosophical Library, 1972), xxi.

25. Mary Morain, "For the Newcomer to General Semantics," in *Enriching Professional Skills Through General Semantics*, ed. Mary Morain (San Francisco: International Society for General Semantics, 1986), x.

26. Alice P. Cherbeneau, "Bringing Up the Family Semantically," in Morain, *Enriching Professional Skills Through General Semantics*, 280.

27. Steve Allen, foreword to *Thinking Creatically*, ed. Kenneth G. Johnson (Englewood, NJ: Institute of General Semantics, 1994), ix.

28. Katherine Liepe-Levinson and Martin H. Levinson, "A General Semantics Approach to School-Age Bullying," *ETC: A Review of General Semantics* 62, no. 1 (January 2005): 15–16.

29. Harry L. Weinberg, *Levels of Knowing and Existence* (New York, Harper, 1959), 10.

30. Ibid., 12.

31. Susan Presby Kodish and Bruce I. Kodish, *Drive Yourself Sane: Using the Uncommon Sense of General Semantics*, rev. 2nd ed. (Pasadena, CA: Extensional Publishing, 2001), 20.

32. Stuart Chase, "Korzybski and Semantics," *The Saturday Review*, June 19, 1954, 48.

33. James D. French, "Time-Binding: To Build a Fire," *ETC: A Review of General Semantics* 46, no. 3 (Fall 1989): 196.

34. Martin H. Levinson, "General Semantics and Emotional Intelligence," *ETC: A Review of General Semantics* 65, no. 3 (July 2008): 249.

35. Wendell Johnson, "Do You Know How to Listen?," *ETC: A Review of General Semantics* 7, no. 1 (Autumn 1949): 6.

36. Mitsuko Saito-Fukunaga, "General Semantics and Intercultural Communication," *ETC: A Review of General Semantics* 46, no. 4 (Winter 1989): 297.

37. Katherine Liepe-Levinson and Martin H. Levinson, "Glossing Over Feminism: A General Semantics Critique," *ETC: A Review of General Semantics* 52, no. 4 (Winter 1995–96): 440.

38. Andrew Lohrey, "General Semantics and Semiotics," *ETC: A Review of General Semantics* 43, no. 4 (Winter 1986): 368.

39. George Doris, "Korzybski and Neurolinguistic Programming," *General Semantics Bulletin* 50 (1983): 142.

40. Milton Dawes, "Management of Stress," *ETC: A Review of General Semantics* 47, no. 2 (Summer 1990): 193.

41. Jeremy Klein, "GS/SF," *ETC: A Review of General Semantics* 59, no. 3 (Fall 2002): 244.

42. Norman T. Newton, *An Approach to Design* (Cambridge, MA: Addison-Wesley, 1951), 27–28.

43. James T. McCay, *The Management of Time* (Englewood Cliffs, NJ: Prentice-Hall, 1959), 57.

44. Oliver Bloodstein, "General Semantics and Modern Art," *ETC: A Review of General Semantics* 1, no. 1 (August 1943): 23.

45. Dale Winslow and Lance Strate, "Poetry Ring," *ETC: A Review of General Semantics* 66, no. 3 (July 2009): 349.

Chapter 7. General Semantics and Emotional Intelligence
1. Peter D. Salovey and John D. Mayer, "Emotional Intelligence," *Imagination, Cognition, and Personality* 9 (1990): 185–211.

2. Daniel Goleman, *Emotional Intelligence: The 10th Anniversary Edition* (New York: Bantam, 2005), ix–x.

3. Ibid., xii.

4. Ibid., xiii.

5. Information in this section has been condensed from "What Are Emotions For?," in Daniel Goleman, *Emotional Intelligence: The 10th Anniversary Edition* (New York: Bantam, 2005), 3–12.

6. Erasmus of Rotterdam, *In Praise of Folly*, trans. Eddie Radice (London: Penguin, 1971), 87.

7. Goleman, *Emotional Intelligence*, 43–44.

8. Ibid., 44.

9. For a more thorough discussion of this subject see Susan Presby Kodish and Bruce I. Kodish, *Drive Yourself Sane: Using the Uncommon Sense of General Semantics*, rev. 2nd ed. (Pasadena, CA: Extensional Publishing, 2001), 100–111.

Chapter 8. General Semantics and Media Ethics
1. John C. Merrill, *Journalism Ethics: Philosophical Foundations for News Media* (New York: St. Martin's, 1997), 155.

2. Kenneth G. Johnson, *General Semantics: An Outline Survey*, 3rd rev. ed. (Fort Worth, TX: Institute of General Semantics, 2004), 21.

3. Ibid., 21.

4. S. I. Hayakawa, *Language in Thought and Action*, 5th ed. (New York: Harcourt Brace, 1990), 30.

5. Stuart Chase, *The Tyranny of Words* (New York: Harcourt Brace, 1938), 21.

6. Merrill, *Journalism Ethics*, 168.

7. Gregg Hoffmann and Paul D. Johnston, *Mapping the Media: A Media Literacy Guidebook* (Whitefish Bay, WI: M&T Communications, 1997), 16.

8. Charles G. Russell and Paul Many, "Using General Semantics Principles in the Basic News Reporting Classroom," *ETC* 50, no. 3 (Fall 1993): 294.

9. Ibid., 294–295.

10. Merrill, *Journalism Ethics*, 171–172.

Chapter 11. Sorting Out the Persian Gulf Naming Dispute

1. Kenneth G. Johnson, *General Semantics: An Outline Survey*, 3rd rev. ed. (Fort Worth, TX: Institute of General Semantics, 2004), 9.

2. Ibid., 21.

3. Gerardus Mercator, "1541 World Map showing the *Sinus Persicus, nunc Mare de Balsera* ('Persian Gulf, now Sea of Basra')," *Harvard University Image Delivery Service*, accessed August 20, 2012, http://nrs.harvard.edu/urn.3:hul.eresource: mercator.

4. Gerardus Mercator, "Ausschnitt 25 der Weldarte 1569," *Wilhelmkruecken.de*, accessed August 18, 2012, http://www.wilhelmkruecken.de/ADUSUM/25.htm.

5. Abraham Ortelius, "1570 map showing the label *Mare El Catif, olim Sinus Persicus*," *Cartographicarts.com*, accessed August 10, 2010; site now discontinued, http://www.cartographicarts.com??popup.html ?img=E4167A.

6. Kaveh Farrokh, "Iran Heritage," *Kavehfarrokh.com*, accessed August 18, 2012, http://www.iran-heritage.org/interestgroups/history-article2.htm.

7. Sam Jones, "Airlines must say 'Persian Gulf' or face Iranian airspace ban," *guardian.co.uk*, February 22, 2010, http://www.guardian.co.uk/world/2010/feb/ 22/iran-airlines-persian-gulf.

8. Simiak D. Ahi, "Persian Gulf Day," *blogspot.com*, July 16, 2005, http://persiangulfday.blogspot.com/2005/07/national-day-of-persian-gulf.html.

9. United Nations Group of Experts on Geographical Names, "Historical, Geographical and Legal Validity of the Name: PERSIAN GULF," *UN.org*, April 4, 2006, http://unstats.un.org/unsd/geoinfo/ungegn/docs/23-gegn/wp/gegn23wp61.pdf.

10. CNN World, "Name game stokes U.S.-Iranian tensions," *CNN.com*, January 24, 2008, http//articles.cnn.com/2008-01-24/...f-20-second-videotape?-s=PM:WORLD.

11. Gary G. Sick and Lawrence G. Potter, eds., *The Persian Gulf at the Millennium: Essays in Politics, Economy, Security, and Religion* (New York: Palgrave Macmillan, 1997), 8.

12. National Geospatial Intelligence Agency, "NGA Geonames Search-OGC

Viewer," *NGA.mil*, accessed August 18, 2012, http://geonames.nga.mil/ggmaviewer.

13. PBS NewsHour, "Bin Laden's 1996 Fatwa," *PBS.org*, August 1996, http://www.pbs.org/newshour/terrorism/international/fatwa/-1996.html.

14. Darrell Christian, Sally Jacobsen, and David Minthorn, eds., *The Associated Press 2009 Stylebook* (New York: Basic Books, 2009), 211.

15. Karolyn Chowning, "Google Earth Under fire From Iranians for Renaming Persian Gulf the 'Arabian Gulf,'" *voices.yahoo.com*, June 16, 2010, http://www.associatedcontent.com/article/2422778/google_earth_under_fire_from_iranians.html?cat=37.

16. National Geographic Society, "Persian Gulf, Persian Gulf states – National Geographic Style Manual," *NGS.org*, accessed August 18, 2012, http://stylemanual.ngs.org/home/P/persian-gulf.

17. Nasser Karimi and Beth Gardiner, "For the Freedom of Iran: June 2006," *blogspot.com*, June 14, 2006, http//forthefreedomofiran.blogspot.com/2006_06_01_archive.html.

18. International Hydrographic Organization, "Limits of Oceans and Seas, Special Publication 23, Third Edition 1953," accessed August 18, 2012, *IHO.int*, http://www.iho-ohi.net/iho_pubs/ standard/S-23/S23_1953.pdf.

19. SOS Iran, "Immediate and unconditional deletion of Arabian Gulf from Google Earth Petition," *PetitionOnline.com*, February 19, 2008, http://www.petitiononline.com/sos02082/petition.html.

20. John Gravois, "The Agnostic Cartographer – John Gravois," *Washington Monthly*, July/August 2010, http://www.washingtonmonthly.com/features/2010/1007.gravois.html.

21. Ibid.

22. Karolyn Chowning, "Google Earth Under Fire From Iranians for Renaming Persian Gulf the 'Arabian Gulf,'" *voices.yahoo.com*, June 16, 2010, http://www.associatedcontent.com/article/2422778/google_earth_under_fire_from_iranians.html?cat=37.

Chapter 12. Alfred Schweitzer and Alfred Korzybski: Champions of Humanity
1. Albert Schweitzer, *Out of My Life and Thought* (Baltimore: The Johns Hopkins University Press, 1998), 201.

2. Ibid., 236.
3. Ibid., 88.
4. Ibid., 224.
5. Ibid., 91.

6. Alfred Korzybski, *Manhood of Humanity,* 2nd ed. (Lakeville, CT: The International Non-Aristotelian Publishing Company, 1950), 1–2.

7. Wendell Johnson, *People in Quandaries: The Semantics of Personal Adjustment* (New York: Harper, 1946), 14.

Chapter 13. How Science Should Be Done: Insights from Santiago Ramón y Cajal

1. Santiago Ramón y Cajal, *Advice for a Young Investigator,* trans. Neely Swanson and Larry W. Swanson (Cambridge, MA: MIT Press, 1999), 2.
2. Ibid., 3.
3. Ibid., 7.
4. Ibid., 10.
5. Ibid., 17.
6. Ibid., 19.
7. Ibid., 24.
8. Ibid., 29.
9. Ibid., 44.
10. Ibid., 48.
11. Ibid., 50.
12. Ibid., 62.
13. Ibid., 54.
14. Ibid., 72.
15. Ibid., 75.
16. Ibid., 78.
17. Ibid., 86.
18. Ibid., 89–90.
19. Ibid., 94.
20. Ibid., 101.
21. Ibid., 111–112.
22. Ibid., 117.
23. Ibid., 121.
24. Ibid., 125.
25. Ibid., 129.
26. Ibid., 133.

27. Ibid., 140–141.
28. Ibid., 146.
29. Ibid., 148.

Chapter 14. GS Wisdom from Wendell Johnson

1. Wendell Johnson, *Your Most Enchanted Listener* (New York: Harper, 1956), 9.

2. Ibid., 50.
3. Ibid., 75.
4. Ibid., 71.
5. Ibid., 159.
6. Ibid., 165.
7. Ibid., 167.
8. Ibid., 171.
9. Ibid., 171.
10. Ibid., 175.
11. Ibid., 184.
12. Ibid., 185–186.
13. Ibid., 185.

Bibliography

Allen, Steve. Foreword to *Thinking Creatically*. Edited by Kenneth Johnson. Englewood, NJ: Institute of General Semantics, 1994.

Anstendig, Linda. "Building Critical Thinking Into a Freshman Writing Course." In *Thinking Creatically*, edited by Kenneth G. Johnson, 211-219. Englewood, NJ: Institute of General Semantics, 1991.

Ashley, Leonard R. N. "Bordering on the Impossible." *ETC* 61, no. 2 (April 2004): 343–348.

Ball, Howard, and Mildred Vasan, eds. *The USA Patriot Act: A Reference Handbook*. Santa Barbara, CA: ABC-CLIO, 2004.

Ballard, Robert D. *The Discovery of the Titanic*. New York.: Grand Central, 1995.

Bar-On, Reuven, J. G. Maree, and M. J. Elias, eds. *Educating People to be Emotionally Intelligent*. Portsmouth, NH: Heinemann Educational Publishers, 2005.

Barratt, Nick. *Lost Voices from the Titanic*. New York: Palgrave, 2010.

Barrett, Lisa Feldman, and Peter Salovey. *The Wisdom of Feeling: Psychological Processes in Emotional Intelligence*. New York: Guilford Press, 2002.

Beesley, Lawrence. *The Loss of the S.S. Titanic: Its Story and Its Lessons*. Boston: Houghton Mifflin, 2000.

Bentley, Wilson J. "General Semantics for Engineers?!," *ETC: A Review of General Semantics* 61, no. 4 (December 2004): 64-68.

Berman, Sanford I., ed. *Logic and General Semantics: Writings of Oliver L. Reiser and Others*. San Francisco, CA: International Society for General

Semantics, 1989.

Bloodstein, Oliver. "General Semantics and Modern Art." *ETC: A Review of General Semantics* 1, no. 1 (August 1943): 12-23.

Bois, J. Samuel. *Explorations in Awareness.* New York: Harper & Row, 1957.

Brewster, Hugh, and Laurie Coulter. *888½ Amazing Answers to Your Questions About the Titanic.* Toronto: Madison Press, 1998.

Brinkley, Alan. *American History: A Survey.* New York: McGraw Hill, 1999.

Brooke, John Hedley. *Science and Religion: Some Historical Perspectives.* Cambridge: Cambridge University Press, 1991.

Brown, David. *The Last Log of the Titanic.* New York, McGraw-Hill, 2001.

Browne, Janet. *Charles Darwin: The Power of Place.* New York: Knopf, 2002.

Butler, Daniel Allen. *"Unsinkable": The Full Story.* Mechanicsburg, PA: Stackpole, 1998.

Caruso, David, R., and Peter Salovey. *The Emotionally Intelligent Manager: How to Develop the Four Key Skills of Leadership.* San Francisco: Jossey-Bass, 2001.

Chase, Stuart. "Korzybski and Semantics." *The Saturday Review,* June 19, 1954.

————. *The Tyranny of Words.* New York: Harcourt Brace, 1938.

Cherbeneau, Alice P. "Bringing Up the Family Semantically." In *Enriching Professional Skills Through General Semantics,* edited by Mary Morain, 280-285. San Francisco, CA: International Society for General Semantics, 1986.

Chisholm, Francis P. *Introductory Lectures on General Semantics.* Lakeville, CT: Institute of General Semantics, 1956.

Christian, Darrell, Sally Jacobsen, and David Minthorn, eds. *The Associated Press 2009 Stylebook.* New York: Basic Books, 2009.

Cohen, Carl, and James P. Sterba. *Affirmative Action and Racial Preference: A Debate (Point/Counterpoint).* New York: Oxford, 2003.

Colling, Richard G. *Random Designer.* Bourbonnais, IL: Browning Press, 2004.

CNN World. "Name game stokes U.S.-Iranian tensions." *CNN.com.* January 24, 2008. http//articles.cnn.com/2008-01-24/...f-20-second-videotape?-s=PM:WORLD.

C-SPAN. "C-SPAN 2009 Historians Presidential Leadership Survey." *C-SPAN.org.* http://legacy.c-span.org/PresidentialSurvey/.

Cox, Stephen. *The Titanic Story: Hard Choices, Dangerous Decisions.* Chicago, Open Court, 1999.

Davie, Michael. *The Death and Life of a Legend.* New York: Knopf, 1986.

Davis, Kenneth C. *Don't Know Much About History: Everything You Need to Know About American History but Never Learned.* New York: Perennial, 2003.

Dawes, Milton. "General Semantics Guides Toward Better Futures." *General Semantics Bulletin* 74-75, (2007/2008): 84-86.

———. "Management of Stress." *ETC: A Review of General Semantics* 47, no. 2 (Summer 1990): 193-194.

Doris, George. "Korzybski and Neurolinguistic Programming." *General Semantics Bulletin* 50 (1983): 141-148.

Eaton, John P. and Charles A. Haas. *Titanic: Destination Disaster: The Legends and the Reality,* rev. ed. New York: Norton, 1998.

Ellis, Albert. *How to Live With a Neurotic.* New York: Crown, 1975.

———. *How to Stubbornly Refuse to Make Yourself Miserable About Anything—Yes, Anything.* New York: Lyle Stuart, 1995.

Ellis, Albert, and Robert A. Harper. *A New Guide to Rational Living.* Hollywood, CA: Wilshire, 1975.

Erasmus of Rotterdam. *In Praise of Folly.* Translated by Eddie Radice. London: Penguin, 1971.

Exton, William Jr. "Managerial Judgment and Critical Thinking." In *Thinking Creatically,* edited by Kenneth G. Johnson, 33-39. Englewood, NJ: Institute of General Semantics, 1991.

Ferngren, Gary B., ed. *The History of Science and Religion in the Western Tradition: An Encyclopedia.* New York: Garland, 2000.

Finocchiaro, Maurice A. *The Galileo Affair; A Documentary History*. Berkeley, CA: University of California Press, 1989.

Flach, Sixten E. "General Semantics in Technical Assistance Work." *ETC: A Review of General Semantics* 24, no. 3 (September 1967): 335-340.

French, James D. "Time-Binding: To Build a Fire." *ETC: A Review of General Semantics* 46, no. 3 (Fall 1989): 194-196.

Goleman, Daniel. *Emotional Intelligence: The 10th Anniversary Edition*. New York: Bantam, 2005.

Gould, Stephen J. *Rock of Ages: Science and Religion in the Fullness of Life*. New York: Ballantine, 1999.

Gravois, John. "The Agnostic Cartographer." *Washington Monthly*. July/August 2010. http://www.washingtonmonthly.com/features/2010/1007.gr avois.html.

Greene, Ross. *The Explosive Child: A New Approach for Understanding and Parenting Easily Frustrated, Chronically Inflexible Children*. New York: Quill, 2001.

Hayakawa, S. I. *Language in Action*. New York: Harcourt, Brace & World, 1941.

―――. *Language in Thought and Action*, 5th ed. New York: Harcourt Brace, 1990.

Heyer, Paul. *Titanic Legacy: Disaster as Media Event and Myth*. Westport, CT: Praeger, 1995.

Hines, Stephen W. *Titanic: One Newspaper, Seven Days, and the Truth that Shocked the World*. Naperville, IL: Cumberland House, 2011.

Hoffmann, Gregg, and Paul D. Johnston. *Mapping the Media: A Media Literacy Guidebook*. Whitefish Bay, WI: M&T Communications, 1997.

Howells, Richard. *The Myth of the Titanic*. New York: St. Martin's Press, 1999.

International Hydrographic Organization. "Limits of Oceans and Seas, Special Publication 23, Third Edition 1953." *IHO.int*. http://www.iho-ohi.net/iho_pubs/standard/S-23/S23_1953.pdf.

Johnson, Kenneth G. *General Semantics: An Outline Survey*, 3rd rev. ed. Fort Worth, TX: Institute of General Semantics, 2004.

Johnson, Nicholas. *What Do You Mean and How Do You Know?* Morrisville, NC: Lulu Press, 2009.

Johnson, Paul M. *A History of the American People.* New York: Harper Perennial, 1999.

Johnson, Wendell. "Do You Know How to Listen?." *ETC: A Review of General Semantics* 7, no. 1 (Autumn 1949): 3-8.

———. *People in Quandaries: The Semantics of Personal Adjustment.* Concord, CA: International Society for General Semantics, 2002.

———. *Your Most Enchanted Listener.* New York: Harper, 1956.

Jones, Sam. "Airlines must say 'Persian Gulf' or face Iranian airspace ban." *Guardian.co.uk.* February 22, 2010. http://www.guardian.co.uk/world/2010/feb/22/iran-airlines-persian-gulf.

Kinzer, Stephen. *Overthrow: America's Century of Regime Change From Hawaii to Iraq.* New York: Times Books, 2006.

Klein, Jeremy. "GS/SF." *ETC: A Review of General Semantics* 59, no. 3 (Fall 2002): 244.

Kodish, Bruce I. "Psycho-Logical Fate and Freedom." *ETC: A Review of General Semantics* 62, no. 4 (October 2005): 352-362.

Kodish, Susan Presby, and Bruce I. Kodish. *Drive Yourself Sane: Using the Uncommon Sense of General Semantics,* rev. 2nd ed. Pasadena, CA: Extensional Publishing, 2001.

Kodish, Susan Presby, and Robert P. Holston, eds. *Developing Sanity in Human Affairs.* Westport, CT: Greenwood, 1998.

Korzybski, Alfred. "General Semantics, Psychiatry, Psychotherapy, and Prevention." In *General Semantics and Psychotherapy,* edited by Isabel Caro and Charlotte Schuchardt Read, 19-39. Brooklyn, NY: Institute of General Semantics, 2003.

———. *Manhood of Humanity,* 2nd ed. Lakeville, CT: Institute of General Semantics, 1950.

————. *Science and Sanity, An Introduction to Non-Aristotelian Systems and General Semantics*, 5th ed. Englewood, NJ: Institute of General Semantics, 1994.

————. *Science and Sanity: An Introduction to Non-Aristotelian Systems and General Semantics*. Lancaster, PA: International Non-Aristotelian Library Publishing Company, 1933.

Lauer, Rachel. "General Semantics and the Future of Education." *ETC: A Review of General Semantics* 24, no. 4 (December 1967): 301-401.

Lee, Irving J. *How to Talk with People*. New York: Harper & Row, 1952.

————. *Language Habits in Human Affairs*, 2nd ed. Concord, CA: International Society for General Semantics, 1994.

————. *The Language of Wisdom and Folly*. San Francisco: International Society for General Semantics, 1949.

Levinson, Martin H. "Albert Schweitzer and Alfred Korzybski: Twentieth Century Champions of Humanity." *ETC: A Review of General Semantics* 66, no. 1 (January 2009): 84-90.

————. "Alfred Korzybski and Rational Emotive Behavior Therapy." *ETC: A Review of General Semantics* 67, no. 1 (January 2010): 55-63.

————. "Crazy Talk, Stupid Talk—Redux." *ETC: A Review of General Semantics* 63, no. 1 (April 2006): 67-76.

————. "Democracy Here is Not Necessarily Democracy There." *ETC: A Review of General Semantics* 63, no. 2 (April 2006): 215-216.

————. *The Drug Problem: A New View Using the General Semantics Approach*. Westport, CT: Praeger, 2002.

————. "Examining Five 'Over/Under-Defined' Terms Used in American Political Discourse." *ETC: A Review of General Semantics* 65, no. 2 (April 2008): 134-140.

————. "Examining Ten Commonly Accepted Verbal Maps of American History." *ETC: A Review of General Semantics* 66, no. 4 (October 2009): 364-370.

————. "A General Semantics Analysis of the *RMS Titanic* Disaster." *ETC: A Review of General Semantics* 69, no. 2 (April 2012): 141-156.

————. "General Semantics And . . .." *ETC: A Review of General Semantics* 67, no. 2 (April 2010): 127-143.

————. "General Semantics and Emotional Intelligence." *ETC: A Review of General Semantics* 65, no. 3 (July 2008): 243-251.

————. "General Semantics and Media Ethics." *ETC: A Review of General Semantics* 64, no. 3 (July 2007): 255-260.

————. "How Science Should be Done: Insights from Santiago Ramón y Cajal." *ETC: A Review of General Semantics* 68, no. 1 (January 2011): 56-62.

————. "Mapping the Persian Gulf Naming Dispute." *ETC: A Review of General Semantics* 68, no. 3 (July 2011): 279-287.

————. "People in Quandaries: Sixty Years Later." *ETC: A Review of General Semantics* 63, no. 3 (July 2006): 290-298.

————. *Practical Fairy Tales for Everyday Living.* Lincoln, NE: iUniverse, 2007.

————. "Science Versus Religion: A False Dichotomy." *ETC: A Review of General Semantics* 63, no. 4 (October 2006): 422-429.

————. *Sensible Thinking for Turbulent Times.* Lincoln, NE: iUniverse, 2006.

————. "Using GS to Enhance Organizational Leadership." *ETC: A Review of General Semantics* 62, no. 3 (July 2005): 250-260.

————. "Your Most Enchanted Listener: GS Wisdom from Wendell Johnson." *ETC: A Review of General Semantics* 65, no. 4 (October 2008): 337-342.

Liepe-Levinson, Katherine, and Martin H. Levinson. "A General Semantics Approach to School to School-Age Bullying." *ETC: A Review of General Semantics* 62, no. 3 (July 2005): 4-16.

————. "Glossing Over Feminism: A General Semantics Critique." *ETC: A Review of General Semantics* 52, no. 4 (Winter 1995-96): 440-454.

Lindberg, David C., and Ronald L. Numbers, eds. *God and Nature: Historical Essays on the Encounter between Christianity and Science.* Berkeley, CA: University of California Press, 1986.

Loewen, James W. *Lies My Teacher Told Me: Everything Your American History*

Textbook Got Wrong. New York: Simon & Schuster, 1996.

Lohrey, Andrew. "General Semantics and Semiotics." *ETC: A Review of General Semantics* 43, no. 4 (Winter 1986): 368-373.

Lord, Walter. *A Night to Remember.* New York: Bantam, 1997.

————. *The Night Lives On.* New York: Morrow, 1986.

Lynch, Don. *Titanic: An Illustrated History.* New York: Hyperion, 1992.

Magee, John. *The General Semantics of Wall Street.* Springfield, MA: John Magee, 1958.

Marcus, Geoffrey. *The Maiden Voyage.* New York: Viking, 1969.

Marsden, George M. *Understanding Fundamentalism and Evangelicalism.* Grand Rapids, MI: Eerdmans, 1991.

Matsen, Brad. *Titanic's Last Secrets.* New York: Twelve, 2008.

McCay, James T. *The Management of Time.* Englewood Cliffs, NJ: Prentice-Hall, 1959.

Merrill, John C. *Journalism Ethics: Philosophical Foundations for New Media.* New York: St. Martin's Press, 1997.

Morain, Mary. "For the Newcomer to General Semantics." In *Enriching Professional Skills Through General Semantics,* edited by Mary Morain, x-xviii. San Francisco, CA: International Society for General Semantics, 1986.

Moran, Terence P. "Media Ecology is General Semantics Writ Large." *General Semantics Bulletin* 74-75, (2007/2008): 38-40.

Morison, Samuel Eliot. *The Oxford History of the American People.* London: Oxford University Press, 1965.

Newton, Norman T. *An Approach to Design.* Cambridge, MA: Addison-Wesley, 1951.

Nierenberg, Gerard I. *The Complete Negotiator.* New York: Nierenberg & Zeif, 1986.

Nowlis, Helen. *Drugs Demystified.* Paris: UNESCO, 1975.

Parkhurst, Eleanor. "Some Implications of General Semantics Methodology for Social Work." *ETC: A Review of General Semantics* 61, no. 4

(December 2004): 639-648.

PBS NewsHour. "Bin Laden's 1996 Fatwa." *PBS.org*. August 1996. http://www.pbs.org/newshour/terrorism/international/fatwa/-1996.html.

Pelligrino, Charles R. *Ghosts of the Titanic*. New York: Morrow, 2000.

Postman, Neil. *Building a Bridge to the Eighteenth Century*. New York, Knopf, 1999.

————. *Crazy Talk, Stupid Talk: How We Defeat Ourselves by the Way We Talk—and What to Do About It*. New York: Delacorte, 1976.

Principe, Lawrence M. *Science and Religion*. DVD. Chantilly, VA: The Teaching Company, 2006.

Ramón y Cajal, Santiago. *Advice for a Young Investigator*. Translated by Neely Swanson and Larry W. Swanson. Cambridge, MA: MIT Press, 1999.

Russell, Charles G., and Paul Many. "Using General Semantics Principles in the Basic News Reporting Classroom." *ETC: A Review of General Semantics* 50, no. 3 (Fall 1993): 287-295.

Saito-Fukunaga, Mitsuko. "General Semantics and Intercultural Communication." *ETC: A Review of General Semantics* 46, no. 4 (Winter 1989): 295-297.

Salovey, Peter, and John D. Mayer. "Emotional Intelligence." *Imagination, Cognition, and Personality* 9 (1990): 185–211.

Salovey, Peter, Marc A. Brackett, and John D. Mayer. *Emotional Intelligence: Key Readings on the Mayer and Salovey Model*. Port Chester, NY: DUDE Publishing, 2004.

Scardilli, Frank. "How Just is Our System of Justice?." Presentation at the "Across the Generations Conference: Legacies of Hope and Meaning," New York, September 13, 2009.

Schweitzer, Albert. *Out of My Life and Thought*. Baltimore: The Johns Hopkins University Press, 1998.

————. *The Philosophy of Civilization: Part 1, The Decay and the Restoration of Civilization; Part 2, Civilization and Ethics*. Whitefish, MT: Kessinger Publishing, 2010.

Scott, Eugenie C. *Creationism vs. Evolutionism: An Introduction*. Westport, CT: Greenwood Press, 2004.

Shenkman, Richard, and Kurt Rieger. *One-Night Stands with American History*. New York, Perennial, 2003.

Sick, Gary G., and Lawrence G. Potter, eds. *The Persian Gulf at the Millennium: Essays in Politics, Economy, Security, and Religion*. New York: Palgrave Macmillan, 1997.

Solomon, Robert C. *True to Our Feelings*. New York: Oxford, 2006.

St. Augustine. *Confessions*. Translated by R. S. Pine-Coffin. New York: Penguin Books, 1961.

United Nations Group of Experts on Geographical Names. "Historical, Geographical and Legal Validity of the Name: PERSIAN GULF." *UN.org*. April 4, 2006. http://unstats.un.org/unsd/geoinfo/ungegn/docs/23-gegn/wp/gegn23wp61.pdf.

Wade, Wyn Craig. *The Titanic: End of a Dream*. New York, Penguin, 1992.

Weinberg, Alvin M. "General Semantics and the Teaching of Physics." *The American Physics Teacher* 7, no. 2 (April 1939): 104-108.

Weinberg, Harry L. *Levels of Knowing and Existence*. New York: Harper, 1959.

Wiegand, Steve. *U.S. History for Dummies*. New York: Wiley, 2001.

Williams, William J. *General Semantics and the Social Sciences*. New York: Philosophical Library, 1972.

Wilson, Frances. *How to Survive the Titanic: The Sinking of J. Bruce Ismay*. New York: HarperCollins, 2011.

Winslow, Dale, and Lance Strate. "Poetry Ring." *ETC: A Review of General Semantics* 66, no. 3 (July 2009): 350-356.

Woods, Thomas E. *The Politically Incorrect Guide to American History*. Washington D.C.: Regnery, 2004.

Zinn, Howard. *A People's History of the United States*. New York: Harper and Row, 1980.

Index

semantics
emotional hijacking, 87–88
emotional intelligence (EI),
 and general semantics, 65–
 66, 85–94
 emotions and brain, 86–88
 empathizing with others,
 92–93
 handling relationships,
 93–94
 knowing one's emotions,
 89–90
 managing one's emotions,
 90–91
 motivating oneself, 91–92
 "thoughts" and "feelings,"
 88–89
 using GS to enhance EI,
 89–94
*Emotional Intelligence: Why
 it Can Matter More than IQ*
 (Goleman), 85
"emotional response," 88
emotional self-management,
 89–94
emotion/thought dichotomy,
 86–89
empathy, 92–93
energy loss, observing, 69
English language and
 dictionary definitions, 14–
 15, 101, 165
Epictetus, 71, 75, 145

Erasmus, 86
Ericson, Leif, 105
*ETC: A Review of General
 Semantics* (journal), 2, 52,
 55
ethics, 58, 65
 See also journalism ethics,
 and general semantics
Eucken, Rudolf Christoph,
 160
evaluational reaction, 64–65,
 66, 88–89, 164
 See also responses, control
 of
evaluational rigidity, in
 language, 17
evil, use of term, 75
evolution, 45–49
*The Evolution of the
 American Flag* (Canby), 107
expectations, and irrational
 beliefs, 82–83
Explorations in Awareness
 (Bois), 65, 94
The Explosive Child
 (Greene), 92
extensional thinking, 32, 66,
 77–78, 90
 See also specific aspects of
 general semantics
Exton, William, Jr., 56

F
fact/inference
  discrimination, 80–81, 97–
  99
fact/opinion dichotomy, 100
facts, as personal
  observations, 14
failure
  and irrational beliefs, 73–
  75
  Johnson's definition of, 10
fallibilism, 26
fanaticism, 25–26
fear, 79, 91
feedback processes, 166–169
feminism, 66–67
financial investing, 59
First Vatican Council (1870),
  46
Flach, Sixten E., 57
Fleet, Frederick, 119
*Flow My Tears, the Policeman
  Said* (Dick), 69
Forcarini, Paolo Antonio, 43
formal rigidity, in language,
  17
formal vs. factual truth, 165
*For the Newcomer to General
  Semantics* (Morain), 62
Founders, on democracy, 34–
  35
Fourth Amendment, 39

freedom of speech, 35
French, James D., 65
Fuller, Buckminster, 94
fundamentalism, 46–49
The Fundamentals (religious
  tracts), 47
Future Shock (Toffler), 2

G
Galileo, 12, 42–44, 50
generalizations, 11
general semantics, practical
  applications of, 52–70
  anthropology, 61
  art appreciation, 70
  bullying, prevention of, 63
  business management, 56
  child rearing, 62–63
  creative thinking, 62
  critical thinking, 63
  dating technique, 41–50,
    82, 93
  design, 69
  education, 52–53
  emotional intelligence,
    65–66
  ethics, 65
  evaluation skills, 64–65, 66
  feminism, 66–67
  human communications,
    54–55
  human energy, efficient use
    of, 69

Horney, Karen, 71
Houston, Sam, 109
How Just is Our System of Justice? (Scardilli), 58
"How to Improve Your Thinking and Communicating Ability" course, 8
How to Talk with People (Lee), 167
human energy, efficient use of, 69
human perception, 103–104
humility, 164–165

I
idealism. *See* IFD disease (Johnson)
IFD disease (Johnson), 9, 27, 74–75, 91–92, 150
illegal aliens, use of term, 32–33
Illinois Historic Preservation Agency, 110
immigration legislation, 32–33
indexing technique
in ethical journalism, 99
explanation of, 151
in handling relationships, 93
of self-talk, 73

See also specific applications of
industrial engineering, 56–57
inertia/inaction, and irrational beliefs, 83–84
inferences, 80–81, 97–99
Institute of General Semantics (IGS), 66, 94
intelligence tests, 18, 27–28, 85
Intelligent Design, 48
intercultural communication, 66
interdisciplinary studies, 61
International Convention for the Safety of Life at Sea (SOLAS), 128–130, 131
International Hydrographic Organization, 140
International Ice Patrol, 131
Introductory Lectures on General Semantics (Chisholm), 53
investing, 59
Iran, 135–136, 138, 139, 140
Iraq, 138
irrational beliefs. *See* Rational Emotive Behavior Therapy (REBT), and general semantics
Islamic Gulf, use of term. *See* Persian Gulf, naming

Kodish, Susan Presby, 64
Korzybski, Alfred
  as contemporary of
    Schweitzer, 144–152
  as founder of general
    semantics, 1, 52, 67, 71
  *General Semantics,
    Psychiatry, Psychotherapy
    and Prevention*, 57–58
  happiness formula, 91–92
  Manhood of Humanity,
    145, 148
  Science and Sanity, 30–31,
    55, 60, 61, 62, 65, 68, 70,
    83, 144–145, 148–149
*Korzybski and General
  Semantics* (Doris), 67
Korzybski and Semantics
  (Chase), 64
Kronprinz Wilhelm (German
  liner), 121

L
labeling via categories, 156–
  157
language
  to be, use of verb, 28
  "blab" language, 102–103
  as driver of thought
    (Wittgenstein), 25
  extremes vs. degrees in
    thought, 150

influence of structuring of,
  150
maladjustment, and
  rigidity in, 16–17
manipulating of, 163
"to me" attitude, 93–94,
  150
polarizing terms in, 99–
  100
and structure of society, 10
and time-binding, 149
verbal vs. visual structure,
  69
written language, 15
See also symbols and
  symbolization
*Language Habits in Human
  Affairs* (Lee), 8, 65
*Language in Action. See now
  Language in Thought and
  Action* (Hayakawa)
*Language in Thought and
  Action* (Hayakawa), 8, 52,
  55, 101–102
*The Language of Wisdom and
  Folly* (Lee), 65
Laplace, Pierre-Simon, 44–45
Lauer, Rachel, 52–53, 59
law of the excluded middle
  (Aristotle), 99–100
leadership, 60
Leclerc, Georges Louis, 44–

Merrill, John C., 53–54, 93,
102–103, 104
See also journalism ethics,
and general semantics
Milgram experiment, 24
Millenarism, 47
Minteer, Catherine, 63
monogenism, 46
Morain, Mary, 62
moral model, on madness,
27–28
Moran, Terence P., 55
multiordinality (*m.o.* terms),
70
multi-valued reasoning, 90–
91, 99–100
Murdoch, William, 121, 123
Mussolini, Benito, 35
musterbation, 76

N
naïve literalism of Bible, 47,
48
*National Geographic Atlas of
the World*, 139
National Geographic Society,
139
*National Geographic Style
Manual*, 139
National Geospatial-
Intelligence Agency, 138
Native Americans and

Columbus, 106
negotiation and general
semantics, 58
neocortex, 87–88
neocreationism, 48
neuroanatomy, 153
neurolinguistic
programming, 67–68
neuro-linguistic reactions, 67
neuro-semantic reactions, 67
*A New Guide to Rational
Living* (Ellis), 72
Newton, Norman T., 69
New York Times, Titanic
story headlines, 118
Nierenberg, Gerard I., 58
Nietzsche, 99
Nineteenth Amendment,
111–112
Nobel Peace Prize, 144
nonverbal communication,
92–93
not-words. *See* word
definitions (not-words)
"Null P" (Tenn), 69

O
observing grid, 69
Oklahoma State University,
56–57
opinions/fact dichotomy,
100

RMS Carpathia, 122, 127

RMS Titanic disaster, general semantics analysis, 115–132

bravery of postal workers, engineers and musicians aboard, 131–132

dating technique and safety regulations, 129–131

importance of accurate assumptions, 120–125

indexing technique, 125–129

journalism ethics and, 117–118, 123–124

unsinkable ship, not really, 116–118

value of delayed reactions, 118–120

role fixation, 26

role structure, 24

Roosevelt, Teddy, 110–111

Ross, Betsy, 107

Rough Riders, 110–111

Russell, Bertrand, 74

Russell, Charles G., 103–104

S

St. Augustine, 41–42

Saito-Fukunaga, Mitsuko, 66

Salovey, Peter, 85

sanity and scientific method, 19–20

Sapir, Edward, 55

Satir, Virginia, 68

Saussure, Ferdinand de, 67

Scardilli, Frank, 58

Schopenhauer, Arthur, 145–146

Schweitzer, Albert, 144–148, 151–152

science

and detection of false beliefs, 26

and scientism, 48

semantic environment of, 23

teaching of, 60, 161

theoretical vs. applied, 155

Science and Sanity (Korzybski), 30–31, 55, 60, 61, 62, 65, 68, 70, 83, 144–145, 148–149

science fiction writing, 68–69

science vs. religion, using dating technique, 41–50

evolution (18th c.), 45–46

faith and reason (4th/5th c.), 41–42

fundamentalism (20th c.), 46–49

Galileo affair (17th c.), 42–44

geology and biblical chronology (18th c.), 44–45

as recent division, 49–50
scientific method
  explanation of, 12
  for exploring solutions,
    82–83
  as extensional approach, 90
  framing useful questions,
    163
  and investigating
    personality, 19–20
  and sanity, 19–20
  as self-corrective, 16
  as time-binding tool, 149–
    150
  See also Cajal, Santiago
    Ramón y
Scopes "Monkey trial"
  (1925), 47
selective abstraction, 76–77,
  101–103, 150
self-discipline, 80–81
self-help methodology, 1, 64
self-management, 68
self-reflexive relationships,
  166–167
self-talk, indexing of, 73
semantic environments
  conflict over purposes, 23–
    24
  elements of, 22–23
  rules of role structure, 24
  words as subject, 25
semantic relaxation, 89–90

semiotics, 67
*Sensible Thinking for
  Turbulent Times*
  (Levinson), 1, 66, 94
Shaw, George Bernard, 123–
  124
signal reactions, 30, 90
sloganeering, 30
smartness, 27–28
Smith, Edward J., 119–120,
  123, 124
social model, on madness,
  27–28
social sciences, 61–62
social work, 56
society and language, 10
*Some Implications of General
  Semantics Methodology for
  Social Work* (Parkhurst), 56
Sorensen, Ted, 112–113
space-binders, 149
sports and sloganeering, 30
SS Californian (cargo
  steamer), 119, 121–122,
  128
Stalin, Josef, 35
Steno, Nicholas, 44
Strabo, 134
Strate, Lance, 70
Straus, Isidor, 125
stress management, 68
Strong, A. H., 46

The Structure of Magic, I and II (Grinder and Bandler), 68
stupid talk. *See* crazy talk, stupid talk, as dysfunctional communication
stuttering, 65
success, and irrational beliefs, 73–75
suffrage movement, 111–112
suffrage rights, 34–35, 111–112, 123
Supreme Court
 on affirmative action, 37
 on creation science as religious doctrine, 48
 on teaching of evolution, 48
symbols and symbolization, 15, 53–54, 69, 87, 96, 149, 150, 163
 See also language

T
teacher training, 53
technical assistance work (UN), 57
Tenn, William, 69
Thinking Creatically (K. Johnson), 63
time-binding power/capacity, 149

Time-Binding: To Build a Fire (French), 65
The Times Atlas of the World, 139
Titanic. See RMS Titanic disaster, general semantics analysis
Titanic Engineers' Memorial (England), 132
to be, use of verb, 28
Tocqueville, Alexis de, 107
Toffler, Alvin, 2
"to me" attitude, 93–94, 150
toxic situations, 76
Two Treatises on Government (Locke), 34
tyranny of the shoulds. *See* Rational Emotive Behavior Therapy (REBT), and general semantics
The Tyranny of Words (Chase), 52, 55, 102

U
Urban VIII, Pope, 44
undocumented immigrant, use of term, 32–33
United Arab Emirates (UAE), 138
United Nations, 57, 137, 140
University of Iowa, 8
University of Michigan, 37

www.ingramcontent.com/pod-product-compliance
Lightning Source LLC
Chambersburg PA
CBHW072130270326
41931CB00010B/1721